Table of Contents

PREFACE 1

INTRODUCTION 3
    Purpose of the Book..3
    Book Structure...3

CHAPTER ONE
WHEREVER WE GO, WE BRING OURSELVES 5
    The Universal Call for Care-Giving 5
    You Can't Give What You Don't Have...............................5
    Humility 6
    The Gift of Care-Giving 7

CHAPTER TWO
THE THERAPEUTIC POWER OF PERSONAL MEANING
AND THE HUMAN SPIRIT 9
    Treating the Human Spirit:
        A Much Needed Discipline and Art...........................9
    The God Question 10
    Spiritual Therapy Potholes 11
    A Psycho-Spiritual Discipline: Logotherapy 12
    The Challenge of Logotherapy 13
    Job and Logotherapy: Complementary Resources............14

CHAPTER THREE
MODELS OF CARE-GIVING 16
    Learning from Job's Friends..16
    Sorry Comforters 16

Inappropriate God-Talk 18
Counsel for Care-Givers 19
God, the Model Care-Giver 21

CHAPTER FOUR
THE LANGUAGE OF SUFFERING AND CARE-GIVING 28
Piety or Popular Faith 28
Silence: The Sacred Language of Suffering 30
Gut-Level Emotions 31
Lament and Protest 31
Health and Growth Considerations 33
Science Amid Suffering: Lectures in Theology,
    Philosophy, and Morality 33
God-Talk 33
Personal Philosophy 34
Morality 35
Suffering and Science: Mixing Apples and Oranges 35
Justice and Disorientation 36
Mystery 37
Recollection and Story 38
Charismatic Prophecy 40
Contemplation 42
Practical Considerations 43
The Contemplative Dimension of Care-Giving 44
Contemplation Begins at Home 45
Contemplation and Elitism 46
Resources on Contemplation 46
Reconciliation 47
Culmination of the Spiritual Journey 48
Reconciliation: Love in Action 48

CHAPTER FIVE
TRUST AND INTEGRITY: ESSENTIAL CARE-GIVER
DISPOSITIONS 51
Mrs. Job 51
Job's Friends 52
Job 54

God...57
The Path of Trust and Reconciliation........................57

CHAPTER SIX
THE HEALING POSSIBILITIES OF HUMOR 61
Preface 61
Humor for Care-Givers...62
The Comedy of Tragedy (Gallows Humor)........................63
Humor, Paradox, and Imagination......................................64
Mr. and Mrs. Job 65
With Friends Like These... 66
The Friends Eat Their Words..66
Thanks, God, But No Thanks...67
Acceptance..68
Humor Begins at Home..68

CHAPTER SEVEN
THERAPEUTIC APPLICATIONS OF JOB.............................71
Foundational Principles..71
Explicit and Implicit Applications of Job 72
The Role of **Lectio Divina** in the Healing Vocations 72
Lectio Divina in Practice 73
Coping with Questions 73
The Innocent Sufferer 74
Theological Undertones 76
The Angry Sufferer 77
The Depressed Sufferer 78
The Searching Sufferer 79
Different Quotes for Different Folks 81
Vocational Therapy for Care-Givers 82
Lectio Divina in Small But Powerful Doses 83
The Place of **Lectio Divina** in Health-Care and
        Pastoral Care 83
Not for Experts Only 84
Motives for Introducing **Lectio Divina**.............................85

CONCLUSION..88
    Job as Therapy 88

NOTES 89

APPENDIX 1: Suggestions for Further Reading.......................93

"JOB THERAPY" WORKSHOPS 97

APPENDIX 2: Accepting the Embrace of God:
    The Ancient Art of **Lectio Divina** 98

Acknowledgments

This book would not have been possible without the support, insight, care, and fidelity of my wife, Jo-Ann. I am grateful from the heart for the opportunity to share the joy and struggles of the journey with Jo-Ann.

Preface

The book of Job is a story about suffering, human nature, and care-giving that integrates earthy wisdom, mystical profundity, psychological acumen, and dramatic characterizations. In light of the immense suffering that is one of the hallmarks of the twentieth century, it is a story for the times. It is the one book in the Bible, and possibly in all of literature, that is sufficiently universal in scope and values to facilitate ecumenical and secular dialogue on the central psycho-spiritual issues of suffering. One of the admirable aspects of Job as a literary work is that the author was able to communicate so much about a secondary topic, care-giving, as a complement to his main subject, human suffering.

As discussed in a companion work for sufferers, *Where Is God When You Need Him?: Sharing Stories of Suffering with Job and Jesus,* Job is a classic testimony to human potential and the human spirit. A chain is only as strong as its weakest link, which in the area of human development is suffering. If you can affirm and build up this link, all other efforts at personal and professional growth will experience a synergistic effect.

Unfortunately, in neither health-care nor pastoral care has Job been given the practical attention it deserves. In talking to college and professional health-care educators, I am frequently given the impression that they are unaware of Job's practical relevance to the care-giving ministry. There is a preference for more established paradigms of suffering such as the Kübler-Ross stages of death and dying. While these models are helpful and the research enlightening, they generally focus more on psychological rather than spiritual dimensions of suffering and care-giving. To this extent, they are incomplete and unbalanced, and need to be supplemented.

In interactions with educators in the field of pastoral ministry, I frequently find a preference for complex psycho-spiritual models that lack the earthiness, practicality, and versatility of Job. This preference is puzzling when one considers the impressive list of pastoral and psychological commentators on Job, including St. Gregory the Great, St. Thomas Aquinas, Martin Buber, Carl Jung, Gustavo Gutierrez, and Jack Kahn, to name a few. It seems prudent to integrate the complex theoretical models used in academia with the practical wisdom of Job.

Readers will note the usage of the masculine pronoun in reference to God. The numerous references made in the book to the interactions between God and Job flow better under this convention; frequent repetition of the divine name God or Lord in lieu of the masculine pronoun becomes awkward. We appreciate the reader's forbearance and understanding on this sensitive issue.

Introduction

Purpose of the Book

The Art and Vocation of Caring for People in Pain explores the positive and negative models of care-giving found in Job, while chronicling its dramatization of the psycho-spiritual language of suffering and care-giving. It seeks to demonstrate that a dialogue involving the disciplines of health-care, spirituality, and pastoral care is a necessity that can be conducted in an ecumenical manner. Job is a good starting point for this objective because it communicates through the universal language of story.

Book Structure

The Art and Vocation of Caring for People in Pain is composed of seven chapters with the following objectives:

Chapter one affirms the importance of self-understanding and humility in the care-giving ministry. Efforts to understand, counsel, and support sufferers must also be applied to ourselves. Care-givers draw on their own experience of suffering for inspiration and direction in responding to sufferers.

Chapter two explores the importance of personal meaning in suffering and care-giving, while highlighting the pioneering work of logotherapy.

In chapter three, we will explore two paradigms of care-giving contained in the book of Job. First, we will consider the attitudes and behavior of Job's pious friends, who serve as a provocative negative model of care-giving. By reflecting upon the friends' deficiencies, modern care-givers can grow in awareness of the timeless traps and temptations that arise in ministry to the suffering. We will then examine the book's portrayal of God as a positive model of care-giving. This revelation is communicated subtly, becoming apparent only by contemplating the story as a whole. By observing God's presence and absence, God's words and silence, we discover an uncomplicated and practical model for being present and helpful to persons in pain.

In chapter four, we will explore the language of suffering and care-giving dramatized by Job. While everyone's experience of suffering and grieving is unique, there are common elements and a general progression that can be observed. In learning this language, care-givers are better equipped to cope with the intense behaviors and questions that arise in situations of suffering.

In chapter five, we will examine the dispositions of trust and integrity as exemplified by the characters in Job. We will look at the possibilities and pitfalls care-givers face in cultivating these much needed virtues.

Chapter six explores the therapeutic benefits of humor for both sufferers and care-givers. We will cite examples from Job which demonstrate that irony and imagination can give rise to humor amid situations of suffering.

Chapter seven concludes our study with practical suggestions for healing and affirming the human spirit through both implicit and explicit use of the book of Job. We will consider the relevance and practical applications of **lectio divina** in both health-care and pastoral care situations.

The appendix includes the Suggestions for Further Reading, information on the "Job Therapy" program on which the book is based, and an informative and practical article published by Fr. Luke Dysinger, O.S.B. on **lectio divina**.

The author hopes that his work will help the book of Job speak to the hearts of individuals from every culture and creed. Job is the voice of solidarity for care-givers and sufferers. It needs to be heard in today's troubled times.

CHAPTER ONE

Wherever We Go, We Bring Ourselves

The Universal Call for Care-Giving

As we begin our exploration of the psycho-spirituality of suffering and care-giving as dramatized by Job, our ultimate objective is to learn how to do the basics better. These core dispositions and practices include listening, touch, presence, encouragement, prayer or reflection, and the willingness to render humble service. These fundamentals are equally relevant for clergy, family members, friends, therapists, and health-care volunteers and professionals. They apply to the caretaker of the elderly parent as much as to the hospital chaplain. They are necessary for anyone called upon to comfort or assist others in pain. Opportunities for care-giving are present not only in health-care environments, therapy sessions, and pastoral care situations, but at the office, home, socially, and in daily encounters. The call to care-giving is universal because everyone suffers and encounters others who suffer.

You Can't Give What You Don't Have

There is a Latin proverb **"Nemo dat quod non habet"** which translates as "you can't give what you don't possess." If we want to inspire others to personal meaning, self-esteem, and acceptance, we must be aspiring to these ourselves. We must attend to our own spiritual dimension, life perspective, and emotional health. The ancient proverb "Physician, heal thyself" comes to mind.

Our personal experience and perspective on suffering will influence how we respond to the suffering of others. The more conscious we are of our own attitudes and beliefs, the less likely we will be to project them on sufferers and peers. Before we explore things from the sufferer's perspective, we must first consider the fundamental care-giving disposition, humility.

Humility

As we gain care-giving experience, we gradually discover the necessity and value of humility. However unique and indispensable our contribution, we are agents, not originators, of healing. The art of care-giving is learning to be caring, helpful, and present to sufferers without becoming possessive or obstructive of the healing process.

Conversely, the more centered on ourselves we are, the more intrusive we will be as care-givers. Usually we have to experience first-hand the negative consequences of vanity and stubborn self-sufficiency before we learn this valuable lesson. Not surprisingly, humility is a fundamental objective of twelve step spirituality. We can't manage things ourselves; we need to rely in a responsible manner on a higher power. When we lose sight of this truth, we transform ourselves into heroes, martyrs, and eventually scapegoats. We end up frustrated, guilt-stricken, and confused. Alternatively, when we let go of our egotistical, controlling agenda, and accept the best efforts of ourselves and others, we can make peace with situations of suffering, be it our own or another's. This process of reconciliation is difficult, time-consuming, and at times spiritually draining and heartbreaking.

As demonstrated by Job's friends, care-givers can easily get in the way of the therapeutic process. We are confronted with situations, personalities, and temptations to which we are highly vulnerable. Getting out of the way means that we recognize that we are precious instruments, but not the cure, and that we function best when we focus on others rather than ourselves. This spirit of humble service requires the commitment and cooperation of the whole person.

The Gift of Care-Giving

Care-giving is a gift to both care-giver and sufferer. If we approach sufferers as objects or numbers to be cared for, our services will benefit no one. When we act as if we are doing them a favor, our efforts are stripped of sensitivity and graciousness. Conversely, if we treat sufferers with respect and dignity, and thereby convey our belief that in the gift of themselves they are giving us something precious, we will enhance the process of growth and healing for all concerned.

The books written by and about Mother Teresa of Calcutta are very instructive in this matter. She offers psycho-spiritual insights and practical wisdom from which care-givers can profit. She captures in simple stories, sayings, and images the fundamental truths that sophisticated textbooks expand into bulky studies and complex theories. Mother Teresa demonstrates that care-givers can incorporate spirituality into their practice without discriminating against those with different beliefs. Fundamental to this capability is a deep reverence for the dignity, freedom, and uniqueness of every individual. She sets a practical example of holistic care-giving in a pluralistic world. There is power in her words because she lives them, and inspires others to do the same.

Reflection Questions

You Can't Give What You Don't Have

Are there any aspects of care-giving in which you would like to improve and develop? Describe the care-giving skills, virtues, or practices you would like to cultivate.

What steps, actions, and attitudes can you take to facilitate this growth?

Staying Out of the Way

Are there situations in which you project your weaknesses and unresolved conflicts onto persons in need of care and support? Consider examples from both your professional and personal life.

The Spirit of Service

In what small ways can you render the gift of humble service?

CHAPTER TWO

The Therapeutic Power of Personal Meaning and the Human Spirit

Treating the Human Spirit: A Much Needed Discipline and Art

The needs and motivational potential of the human spirit are a fundamental aspect of health-care, pastoral care, and human development. Human beings are healthiest when their faculties of mind, body, and spirit are developed and cared for in an integrated manner.

Efforts to minister to the human spirit need not be grand, strained, or clumsy. Nor are care-givers called to engage in spiritual counseling that is untimely or beyond their competence. I am simply speaking of basic courtesy, respect, and compassion. How would we like to be treated if we were in their position? An accepting, listening, gentle, and (most important) patient-driven approach works best. The beliefs, values, and priorities of the care-giver must be subordinated to those of the patient or loved one.

Inviting religiously-inclined sufferers to talk about their personal beliefs, concerns, and anxieties can contribute to their health, comfort, and peace of mind. For example, if a patient is Buddhist and wishes to be treated as one, the individual's desire should be facilitated and completely respected. If they are nominally Catholic, and prefer to keep religion out of the process, respect their wishes. Our duty is to help individuals fulfill their spiritual objectives and commitments inasmuch as this is therapeutic and practical within the care-giving context. In the words of Viktor Frankl: "However, when a patient stands on the firm ground of religious belief, there can be no objection to making use of the therapeutic effect of his religious convictions and thereby drawing upon his spiritual resources. In order to do so, the psychiatrist may put himself in the place of the patient."[1]

We should bear in mind that even sensitive attempts at spiritual therapy will not be universally welcomed. We will not always say the right thing at the right time. However, if we preface and unite spiritual therapy with loving care and presence, sufferers will know we are on their side, and any mistake in judgment or application will be cushioned by our sincerity and attentiveness.

Therapy for the human spirit must be applied according to the needs of the individual and the competence of the care-giver. We cannot help everyone in every area, nor should we try. However, awareness of basic struggles of the human spirit such as the God question and personal meaning is important for all care-givers, so we shall consider these and suggest resources for further exploration.

The God Question

In western society, potentially volatile issues such as religion and death are frequently consigned to their own little world. If we don't talk about them, they won't spoil the works. This may be prudent at times in the business and political realms, but not in health-care, pastoral care, or certain family situations.

What we will term the God question is comprised of the typical questions raised by sufferers concerning God's relationship to their suffering: "Is God punishing me, or is my suffering the result of natural causes? Why doesn't God heal my child? Why did God permit this?" God questions are raised by patients, families, and care-givers from dispositions ranging from positive/searching to negative/despairing. All questions regarding

God that express the true feelings of patients and families without doing spiritual, psychological, or physical damage can be classified as positive. As exemplified by Job's friends, negative God questions are those that tear persons down and accelerate an ongoing process of interior despair that obstructs the healing process.

God questions become a critical aspect of health-care when they are shown to be affecting the sufferer's or family's well-being. Sufferers who feel God is vindictively punishing them have a serious obstacle to healing in their path. While care-givers can't remove it by themselves (the sufferer must *want* to have it removed), they can listen, provide physical (i.e. touch), emotional, and spiritual support, and gain the sufferer's trust. They can carry on a dialogue with sufferers who are wrestling with God questions and who are looking for communication outlets and personal support.

Spiritual Therapy Potholes

There are negative possibilities in spiritual therapy as in all aspects of health-care. The role or use of spirituality can be exaggerated, distorted, or manipulated. A care-giver can force or misinterpret the sufferer's agenda, and thereby intimidate or embarrass the sufferer and family members. The care-giver can retard the healing process by refusing to acknowledge and listen to the God question. Care-givers struggle with suffering along with the sufferer, and are susceptible to the temptation to project their beliefs and struggles onto the health-care or pastoral care situation. Also, if care-givers are not careful to maintain some emotional distance between themselves and the sufferer, they can be swept away by the grief and confusion, and consequently lose objectivity and heart. Logotherapy, the school of psychology most compatible with Job, suggests strategies and attitudes for building up the human spirit as part of the care-giving vocation.

A Psycho-Spiritual Discipline: Logotherapy

As discussed above, caring for the human spirit is a delicate area which requires common sense, experience, and an open heart and mind. Unfortunately moral and spiritual development topics receive insufficient attention in many college and continuing education curriculums, although this pattern seems to be reversing itself gradually. One of those inspiring this reversal, Austrian psychiatrist Viktor Frankl, has written a vivid testimony to the power of the human will and spirit amid suffering entitled *Man's Search for Meaning.* In this work, Frankl lays the foundation for the school of psychotherapy known as logotherapy. Logotherapy explicitly acknowledges the substantial role the human spirit plays in the healing process. This provides a healthy and refreshing contrast to other twentieth century psychological schools which subordinate the role of the human spirit and downplay the potential contributions of religion and spirituality to personal health. Logotherapy recognizes the importance of a self-motivated and holistic approach to health without denying legitimate medical and psychological therapies. It regards personal meaning as an important component of human health that must be assimilated into the therapy process. In his quest to discover meaning in his suffering, Job dramatizes many of the fundamental values of logotherapy.

The root of logotherapy is the Greek word *logos,* which is the translation of the Hebrew word *dabar* used to describe the word of God. The meaning of *logos* or *dabar* (pronounced da-var) is much more than simply "word." It encompasses an underlying thought, action, and force of will. Unlike in western culture, where a person's word does not necessarily imply an underlying action or thought, *dabar/logos* carried connotations of integrity and wholeness. For the ancient oriental, a word had power to fulfill the objective for which it was spoken because it had the whole person behind it.

It is not coincidental that both logotherapy and *lectio divina* (see chapter seven) use the concept and power of *logos* as a means to personal healing and transformation. *Lectio divina* is a spiritual complement to the more psychologically oriented logotherapy. Logotherapy focuses on *logos* in the generic psycho-spiritual sense of personal meaning. *Lectio divina* conceives of *logos* in the biblical sense of God's word. As will be discussed in chapter seven, it is important in the context of care-giving not to restrict the framework of *lectio divina* to Christian individuals. The four stages of *lectio divina* (reading/listening, meditation/reflection, prayer, and contemplation) are basic human activities that are not exclusive to Judeo-Christian spirituality. With sensitivity and common sense, they can be adapted to care-giving situations involving individuals of other faith traditions. There is enough theological and anthropological common ground in the four stages to merit ecumenical pastoral care and secular health-care usage.

The Challenge of Logotherapy

Are we as care-givers willing to support patients, families, peers, and ourselves in the struggle to find a motivation or word (as defined above) to get us through difficult situations? Such a word may be all that people who are dying or coping with tragedy have to live for. This word may or may not be spiritually related, but that is not the question for care-givers. The question is: Will we treat and build up the whole person by prudently encouraging and if necessary assisting them in their quest to ascribe meaning to their suffering? Such meaning can make a difference in human lives.

Lest we conceive of spiritual therapy as necessarily complex, Job reminds us that what the sufferer desires most is to be listened to, understood, touched, and comforted in practical ways. These manifestations of compassion transcend the boundaries of creed and stimulate solidarity in suffering. We may not have the answers, but we can enter into the pain and therapeutic process in practical, empathetic, and unassuming ways. The gift of ourselves is a touching (literally) contribution to the healing process of the sufferer and ourselves.

Job and Logotherapy: Complementary Resources

As care-givers, we are fortunate to have recourse to logotherapy, an unfolding psycho-spiritual science that provides both a theoretical and a practical base for helping persons discover and give meaning to life and suffering. We are likewise fortunate to have Job, a truly existential work[2] that dramatizes the principles and practices of spiritual therapy. The concepts, images, and values of Job are relevant to individuals from all culture and creeds. The student of Job and logotherapy will find them to be complementary resources for consoling and inspiring the human spirit.

Every culture and creed speaks the language of suffering, albeit in different dialects. The book of Job not only articulates and dramatizes this language, but presents both a right and wrong way to go about care-giving. Before we learn the language, we will examine the contexts in which dialogue develops. In the next chapter, we will examine the contrasting models of care-giving which develop in the book of Job.

Reflection Questions

Personal Meaning

Based on your life vision and experience, how can personal meaning be a dynamic ingredient in the healing process?

In what small but practical way can you help someone rediscover and utilize personal meaning amid a difficult situation?

Is your care-giving vocation or ministry energized by personal meaning?

Spiritual Therapy

To which of the potential traps and temptations (e.g. projection, long-windedness, insensitivity, over-zealousness, dogmatism) inherent in spiritual therapy are you most vulnerable? Can you think of any reasons for your vulnerabilities?

CHAPTER THREE

Models of Care-Giving

Learning from Job's Friends

Chapters one through three of Job provide a foundation for understanding the speeches and conflicts that follow. They constitute a timeless story about suffering that invites readers to relate the words and events to their life. In chapters one and two we meet Job, a prosperous oriental chieftain whom God tests to prove the purity of his motives. Despite suffering complete devastation, including alienation from his wife, his sole remaining family member, Job remains faithful to God. He is joined on the dung heap by three religious friends who express their solidarity through grieving and silence. After the traditional seven day mourning period, Job utters a bitter lament, at which point his friends intervene and try to save Job from himself.

The length, complexity, and repetitive nature of the friends' speeches merits an in-depth study beyond the scope of our commentary. This chapter is designed to survey the themes that are most relevant to the care-giver, while referring the reader to the more extensive commentaries listed in the Suggestions for Further Reading. With this goal in mind, we will ask what the tone, words, and disposition of the friends can teach us about the art and vocation of care-giving and the needs of the sufferer.

Sorry Comforters

In chapter four of Job, we are introduced to Eliphaz the Temanite, the eldest of Job's three friends. After beginning his counsel in a polite and encouraging manner, he gradually introduces the themes on which the friends will harangue Job. For Eliphaz and his friends, prolonged suffering of the obvious kind experienced by Job could only be due to Job's sinfulness. For Job's friends, suffering is always the direct result of sin; mystery plays no role in their explanation of Job's misfortunes. If you want to end your suffering, confess your sins and plead for forgiveness. If you repent and your affliction remains, wait on the Lord; he will vindicate you eventually. Humans are worms before God,[3] and have no claim whatsoever on him. The friends embellish their arguments with a variety of images drawn primarily from nature and Near Eastern culture.

It is important to understand that much of what the friends say is both theologically correct and steeped in human wisdom. In a different scenario and with a different approach, their counsel might have been quite appropriate. There is never a doubt as to their sincerity both in comforting Job and in defending their traditional religious doctrines. Their mistake lies in their overly rational approach, unbridled zeal, and unsympathetic attitude. What is lacking are nuance, compassion, and sensitivity. Examining the mentality underlying their behavior makes it easier to understand their indiscretion.

The friends apply their religious doctrines in an impersonal, mechanical manner. They treat Job's situation as a black and white case which does not require empathy and understanding. They are thereby transformed from model comforters to dispensers of easy answers. They seem afraid or unwilling to enter into Job's pain to the degree necessary to understand his lament.

We become like the friends when we express our sympathy through pious platitudes without trying to do anything, however small, to make the sufferer's situation more bearable. We can rationalize our stoicism and lack of action until we end up in the position of the sufferer. Then, when others respond to us in a similar manner, we get irked and complain.

It is interesting that in the gospels when Jesus speaks of serving God in the person of the suffering individual, he refers to basic acts of kindness: giving a cup of cold water, providing food, visiting the prisoner, binding wounds, going out of one's way for another, sharing one's resources, and comforting the sick person. He speaks primarily of tangible, practical manifestations of compassion and love in action.

Many care-givers worry about what they should do to comfort ill or dying individuals. Simple and sincere responses such as touch, tears, and presence are always appropriate. Second, ask if there is anything they would like to have done for them, or if there is anything they wish to talk about. Supplementing this, tap into your creativity and personal experiences. If you were ill or dying, what would make you feel better? In general terms, what would be your needs?

Inappropriate God-Talk

Insensitive God-talk and simplistic platitudes can become painful burdens for sufferers. Many readers of Job have commented that it was the friends' distorted God-talk and heartless condemnation of Job that led him to perceive God as his adversary. The friends enthusiastically defend God at Job's expense. They sincerely believe they are speaking for God when in reality they are simply projecting their self-serving, retribution-based image of God. They seem totally unaware of their bias and hidden agenda. We think we are immune to such self-deception until a personal blind spot is revealed and we are embarrassed, if not crushed.

Because all human images of God are inevitably prejudiced and imperfect, the comforter must be aware of the temptation to project a self-serving image of God when engaging in religious discussions with suffering individuals. Such an image can camouflage painful self-doubt, guilt, and insecurity, or it can reflect pride, immaturity, or self-centeredness. Sensitive, sufferer-centered conversation and inquiries should mark the care-giver's participation in religious dialogue. This helps the care-giver to understand sufferers' perspectives on God and their misfortune.

Counsel for Care-Givers

If we recognize our capability of emulating the friends, we might consider the following preventive counsels:

1) *Presence*

When we are in the role of comforter, our first duty is to be present to those who are suffering. This implies that we put their needs first and orient ourselves toward helping them through touch, deed, word, or caring presence. We are called to subordinate our needs in a prudent, healthy fashion to accommodate the more urgent needs of the sufferer.

One of the side-effects of this willingness to forget ourselves temporarily is a greater sense of priorities and appreciation of life. When people suffer and we are willing to be there with them at a cost to ourselves, we learn that people are ultimately most important in life, and that life cannot be taken for granted. Learning to treasure or at least make the best of the present moment liberates us from paralyzing anxieties and superfluous concerns. This presence to the present lightens our spirit and makes us more aware of and receptive to the graces of the moment. We can then more easily discover the trivialities, distorted priorities, and unhealthy attitudes which isolate us in cells of self-pity, intolerance, and insecurity.

2) *Projection*

Before you bring out a laundry list of religious or practical wisdom, determine what clothes of the sufferer require cleaning. Very often, the words and deeds offered by care-givers are subconsciously designed to insulate them from the sufferer's pain. We are tempted to project our thoughts, beliefs, values, and experiences onto the sufferer, rather than try to discover and build upon theirs.

There is great wisdom in the expression that we never know what something feels like until we experience it ourselves. While we obviously cannot be familiar with all forms of suffering, we can try to place ourselves in the sufferers' shoes and treat them as we would wish to be treated. This requires prayer, reflection, and common sense. As mentioned above, it includes the simple courtesy of asking sufferers how they would like to be helped, or if there is anything on their mind they'd like to share. A timeless guide to counseling persons in difficult pastoral situations is St. Gregory the Great's *Pastoral Care* (see this chapter's Suggestions for Further Reading). Note that St. Gregory found the book of Job to be rich in pastoral insight, hence his prodigious and still relevant commentary on Job.

3) *God-Talk*

One must be very cautious when talking about God amid people who are suffering. God-talk that tears people down is evangelization in reverse. It is very easy to speak with certitude and confidence about God during prosperous times. However, as biblical sufferers such as Peter, Elijah, and Moses experienced, certain trials can shake us to the core of our faith and cause us to act in a way we would not have foreseen. We never really know how we would react in certain situations, nor how we would perceive God. As a care-giver, all we can do is abstain from judgment of the sufferer and humbly ask God to make us instruments of consolation and healing.

4) *Living from the Heart*

The friends inspire us to pause and reflect upon whether we are living our faith from the head or the heart. While it is necessary to integrate the two, living from the heart requires a deeper level of commitment. It compels and energizes us to fulfill our ministry. As with Job and his friends, when trouble arrives, our gut-feelings about God arise and inner attitudes are revealed. We discover if what we affirm with our mind and our mouths is echoed in the depths of our hearts.

Prayer and praxis (faith in action) are the catalysts of such integration. They are as important for the care-giver as for the sufferer.[4] Our example will be more effective than words in helping sufferers speak, pray, and live from the heart.

5) *Presumption*
Perhaps no aspect of the friends' intolerance is as damaging to Job as their tendency to presume and judge. Here is a person with nothing left but his integrity, yet this is the very focal point of their attack. Imagine the damage they would have done to Job's psyche and confidence in God and himself were he not so steadfast! Their presumption only serves to make Job more determined. Although Job's character is strengthened by his perseverance, the friends' arrogance might also have subtly influenced him to hurl misdirected accusations at God (e.g. that God was Job's adversary rather than advocate).

When we find ourselves tempted to render some judgment or unkind remark against someone who is suffering, we might ask: Where is my negativity coming from? What is my motive for putting this person down? Why do I feel drawn toward this action? Pride and insecurity can compel us to boost ourselves at another's expense. The care-giver who is in touch with the inner self is more capable of ministering sensitively to the inner hurts of others. The more aware I am of my own weaknesses, the less likely I will project them upon others.

Having considered what can go wrong in care-giving, let us now explore a positive model.

God, the Model Care-Giver

A mysterious theophany[5] follows Job's heated discussions with his friends. One aspect of this unforeseen occurrence is the characterization of God as a model care-giver. As we have seen, the friends started out as model care-givers, but got sidetracked by their fears, rigidities, and insecurities.

The God who heals Job is the omnipotent, omniscient, and providential Lord of creation extolled by Job and his friends. Job underscores this in his "acceptance speech" in 42:1-6. More important for Job is that God is a compassionate comforter who listens, inspires, and offers assurance and hope.

The book of Job presents God as a positive model of care-giving through the following characterizations:

1) *God listens and responds to Job's cry with Job's integrity and best interest in mind.*
   God listens, doesn't interrupt, and is not personally offended by Job's harsh accusations. He considers the source and situation. Egocentric concerns neither impede his listening nor dictate his response. When he rebukes Job for his words born of ignorance, we sense it is more out of concern for Job and the truth than to preserve his own reputation. If God were militant (rather than merciful) about the sanctity of his image, would he have twice commended Job for speaking rightly about him?[6] Further, would he have rebuked his apologists, the friends, who showered him with accolades and praise throughout their dialogue with Job?

   Although listening is always a recommended practice, doing it amid situations of suffering can be a difficult proposition. The kind of listening engaged in by God is not a cool, detached effort, but a holistic, intense presence. It must not have been easy for God to hear Job, his pride and joy (as we are), say the things he did. Listening can be painful when we feel consciously or subconsciously that it is at our expense. The true test of listening occurs when we are tired, stressed, or threatened. Care-givers are edified by families who struggle to listen to each other when the suffering of a family member is the direct or indirect subject of conversation.

   It can be quite difficult for care-givers to listen to their peers, supervisors, or subordinates, as well as their patients or loved ones. Care-giving is an intense, potentially draining activity that requires a spirit of camaraderie and communal effort. Without mutual support from our peers and family, we will be susceptible to disillusionment, depression, and apathy.

2) *God doesn't take Job too seriously.*
God has fun with Job in a harmless way while teaching him an important lesson. He is not surprised by any form of human defiance. In lieu of over-reacting, he offers Job the possibility of redeeming his situation through obedience/abandonment to God's will. In a subtle, playful way, he helps Job find meaning and the divine presence in his suffering.

If God had taken Job too seriously, his response might have been harsher and more accusatory. Instead, God understood Job's words in the context in which they were spoken. If God can overlook near-blasphemous speech uttered at his expense, surely we as care-givers can tolerate threatening religious language from persons in pain, whether it is at God's expense or ours. As mentioned in chapter two, fiery God-talk can reflect or beget positive or negative dispositions, depending on the attitudes and reactions of the persons involved.

3) *God educates Job[7] in an experiential manner using analogies, questions, and images.*
God invites Job to contemplate creation as an alternative to approaching it rationally. He speaks to Job in images he can absorb, if not totally comprehend. He paints a picture for Job to see and marvel at. His presence and revelation inspires Job to balance his anthropocentric (i.e. humanity-centered) perspective on life with the divine perspective.

Rather than argue or debate with Job at the level of rational language, God immerses Job in the language of mystery and contemplation. He communicates with Job through images and personal experience of creation rather than theological doctrines. God wants Job to contemplate and participate in the mystery, rather than try to solve it. He refuses to provide answers which would probably satisfy Job only temporarily. Are there any rational answers to suffering that we can apply to all situations, or that satisfy us more than momentarily? With each answer we give or receive, additional questions arise. God avoids the answer game by responding to Job's questions with questions of his own. This not only reflected rabbinic practice of the time, but respected the nature of mystery. It is our response to the questions put to us by suffering, rather than the questions we ask of suffering or God, that ultimately will determine the effect suffering will have on our lives.

How does this translate for care-givers? First, no debate on suffering is likely to be successful when conducted at the level of rational language. If a sufferer tries to engage you at the level of theology or philosophy, the prudent response is usually to listen politely but avoid confrontation. Try to move the conversation to a more personal plane. It is not so much what people say as the images underlying their words that is important.

Second, sensitive use of questions helps both sufferer and care-giver perceive the problem more clearly. Questions invite sufferers to participate in the healing process by reflecting upon and sharing their story. The highly experiential nature of suffering dictates that the therapy which will be most effective for the mind and spirit is that which touches and catalyzes the sufferer's experience.

4) *God believes in Job.*
   If God lacked confidence in Job, he would not have challenged him, let alone appeared to him. Apparently, God sees something in Job that Job overlooked when he was recounting his virtues in his final testimony. God is pleased, but not satisfied with Job. He is not afraid to challenge Job, though he does it with sensitivity, confidence, and creativity. At no point is God ever condescending or manipulative. Even Job's wild claims, warnings, and challenges do not deter God's faith in him.

God's faith in Job inspires care-givers to demonstrate faith in both sufferers and their family. Care-givers must balance this confidence with a realistic assessment of their situation and state of mind. Care-giver confidence can affirm sufferers and inspire them to discover hope and meaning in their plight. If sufferers can't discover implicit meaning in their suffering, they can give it explicit meaning through positive actions and attitudes. In light of these motivational objectives, it is important to keep in mind that we cannot communicate hope and self-confidence to others if we lack these virtues ourselves. Our actions and attitude, rather than words, will be our best witness.

5) *God is patient and persistent.*

Traditionally, God's response to Job in chapters 38-41 is interpreted as two speeches separated by Job's humble (and perhaps fearful) response in verses 40:3-5. There is even a question, debated by biblical scholars, as to whether the same author composed both speeches. Academic questions aside, one insight that could be drawn from these speeches is that the communication and care-giving process is vulnerable to human weakness and limitations, even when God is involved. Perhaps the most graphic illustration of this vulnerability is the story of Jesus healing the blind man in verses 8:22-26 of the gospel of Mark. The first time Jesus rubs mud and spittle on his eyes, the man's sight is restored only partially. For whatever reason, known only to God or perhaps the evangelist, Jesus needs to repeat the healing gesture to restore the man's sight completely. The Lord himself must persevere in care-giving situations where the first effort falls short of its purpose. Fortunately for the followers of Jesus throughout history, he welcomes the opportunity to walk with us one step at a time.

Given Job's response and God's rejoinder in chapters 40-41, it appears as if the element of freedom was not sufficient for God's purposes. Job seems overwhelmed into capitulation.

God's intent was not to intimidate, but to lead Job out of his traditional, retribution-based perspective into a more personal experience of religion. Since God did not wish to win him over by force, he had further educating or leading out to do, which he continues in the speech following Job's initial response.[8]

Based on Job's confession of faith in 42:1-6, God's playful and appreciative description of his power over and delight in chaotic creatures such as the hippopotamus and the crocodile (creatures who share with Job a common creator and an unruly, independent disposition)[9] achieved his purposes. Apparently God wills and delights in the freedom of all creatures, including rebellious souls like Job (and us of course) who are quick to reprimand him when events turn sour. We are indeed blessed that God is patient and has a sense of humor.

No one with experience ever said care-giving or suffering was easy, least of all the biblical authors. Care-giving is an art and a vocation. If you expect to get it right the first time, you are in the wrong business. When encountering human beings, God doesn't necessarily achieve certain objectives immediately. Can we expect it to be any different for us as care-givers?

Reflection Questions

Job's Friends

Do you see yourself in Job's friends? If so, how? What has caused you to exhibit similar attitudes or behaviors?

The Divine Care-Giving Model

Which of the preventive counsels (i.e. presence, projection, God-talk, living from the heart, presumption) strike a chord in you? How might you grow in these areas?

As a model care-giver, God listens, challenges, retains a sense of humor, demonstrates confidence, and is persistent. How have you displayed these dispositions in your encounters, ministry, or profession as a care-giver?

Do you discern a need to improve in any of the above areas? If so, what practical attitudes and actions can you take to foster your development?

When you have suffered, have your care-givers, be they family, friends, pastoral or professional care-givers, resembled the positive model of God or the negative example of Job's friends? Has your understanding of the care you received changed in light of the story of Job? If so, how?

If you have experienced care-givers who remind you of Job's friends, do you feel angry or resentful toward them? How would you describe your feelings? What counsel do you think Job would offer you?

CHAPTER FOUR

The Language of Suffering and Care-Giving

In chapter three, we articulated insights into care-giving drawn from the contrasting approaches of God and Job's friends. Equally relevant to our formation as compassionate care-givers is an understanding of the types and progression of language used by sufferers and care-givers to cope with suffering. Perhaps the most practical aspect of Job for sufferers and care-givers is its portrayal of the process of learning to speak and act with integrity when confronted with suffering. A chronological reading of the book reveals the various stages and characteristics of coping language used by Job and his friends. Further, care-givers and sufferers confronted by disease, illness, deprivation, or tragic loss will discover that Job is a vivid dramatization of the Kübler-Ross stages of death and dying. In this chapter, we will review the hierarchy of coping language dramatized by the book of Job, with an emphasis on its implications for the care-giver.

Piety or Popular Faith

In the prologue, Job speaks the language of piety or popular faith in response to his suffering. He continues to defend and bless God despite his misfortune. This language is articulated in Job and elsewhere in the Bible through proverbs, poems, prayers, and platitudes. There exists a progression of faith inten-

28

sity within this category. For example, in verse 1:21 Job's statements progress in religious depth from the philosophical ("Naked I came from my mother's womb, and naked shall I return there") to the pious ("The Lord gave and the Lord has taken away") to the level of personal faith ("Blessed be the name of the Lord!").

The language of piety is what we are taught to say about God and life, rather than what we necessarily feel or believe at the gut or heart level. Human beings begin at the level of popular faith; it is the seed which requires time and reflection to blossom into mature personal faith. Truths expressed in statements of piety need to be personally affirmed or experienced by the individual. Doses of religion, spirituality, or morality to unwilling sufferers are ill-advised. This is one reason for the preeminence of listening and timely questions in the care-giving ministry.

Job's responses in the prologue are sincere but trite, and we eventually discover that he had not considered their ultimate ramifications. In fairness to Job, and by implication ourselves, how could we expect this? It is characteristic of the language of popular faith that we are not fully aware of the implications of our words. We speak nice-sounding phrases without a deep understanding of what they mean in practical terms. Our language is sincere in intent but lacking in sophistication. Only with experience and reflection do we discover the full implications of the moral values and religious beliefs we profess.

The language of piety is appropriate as an immediate response to suffering. We have not had time to discern and understand our deepest feelings in response to the circumstances. In the long term, popular faith lacks the depth of personal faith and the integration of emotions and experience necessary to cope with difficult circumstances. The language of popular faith is unhealthy only to the extent that it functions as a prolonged denial of one's true feelings (repression) or as an escape from consideration of the deeper implications and demands of religious faith.

Silence: The Sacred Language of Suffering

It is important to note that Job's friends commence their care-giving in the proper manner. They mourn with their whole beings and follow with a prolonged period of silence. The narrator reveals the catalyst of their silence: "...but none of them spoke a word to him; for they saw how great was his suffering."[10] In faithfulness to their senses, the friends are overwhelmed into silence. What could they possibly say that might defuse or improve the situation?

Silence is both an intermediate and a final stage of coping language. Both silence and popular faith have different levels of intensity that vary with the individual and the circumstance. Just as popular faith ideally will yield to deeper, personal faith, so silence can gradually lead toward contemplation. In response to suffering, silence is initially a defensive or coping reaction. Even if we could articulate our feelings, the words would seem hollow and impotent.

In its role as a preliminary stage of coping, silence functions as a fermenting agent on both a conscious and a subconscious level. Job's silence gave him time to gather his thoughts, mobilize his emotions, and formulate his response. While at certain points in the healing process the sufferers do need verbal communication in the form of consolation, counsel, exhortation, or even gentle correction, they have a corresponding need for silence. The appropriate timing and dosage of silence will vary with the individual. On a practical level, silence helps the care-givers to avoid projecting their own agenda onto the sufferer. This allows the sufferers to choose their words or actions without distraction or interference.

Silence provides room for human and divine consolation to penetrate the heart and heal the person interiorly. Silence implies a recognition of the inadequacy of human language and the need for physical, emotional, and spiritual solidarity. It is an indispensable aspect of the therapeutic process for both the sufferer and the care-giver.

Gut-Level Emotions

The anguished Job of the dialogue (chapters 3-31 of Job) speaks the language of gut-level emotions. Any reference to theological doctrines comes from the heart as opposed to the head. In common language, this is the stage of getting something off our chest or out of our system. It is a purging of the emotions ignited by suffering.

Gut-level expression is an important initial step in the therapeutic process. While it is necessary to share our feelings honestly with God and others, such sharing needs to be complemented by listening and contemplation. In the latter activities, the focus is taken off ourselves, which in itself can be therapeutic. Gut-level communication is not sufficiently infused with personal faith to satisfactorily express the individual's total response to suffering. In the words of the popular proverb, faith is more than feelings.

Once gut-feelings are expressed, the sufferers' underlying psycho-spiritual disposition must be discerned. What does their communication convey about their spiritual and emotional state? As Job discovered, such expression of emotions is only the beginning of the healing process. It is primarily a revelation of one's current state rather than an indication of what the future must hold. Both sufferer and care-giver have the freedom to respond in a variety of ways to an emotional outburst. For Job, it was a catalyst and stepping stone to the pivotal questions he was to ask himself and eventually God about the dark realities of life and the meaning of the events that had occurred in his life.

Lament and Protest

The term "lament" is frequently used to describe the intense expression of grief and anguish by biblical characters and authors. A staple of the Hebrew scriptures, especially the psalms and prophets, a lament is an example of gut-level expression amid great suffering and the mysterious silence of God. A lament is composed of intense questions, imperatives, petitions, declarations, and interior and exterior sighs and groans. It is the manner of expression used by Job throughout his speeches. Its simplicity and universal applicability make it a natural form of language for sufferers from a variety of religious perspectives and levels of faith.

We use the word "protest" to describe a lament uttered in a spirit of solidarity with other sufferers. It can be expressed individually or in unison with others. It signifies an expansion of consciousness and a broader scope of concern than simply the self. Job's growing consciousness of the injustice in the world leads him to question retribution doctrine not only in his own situation, but in the many cases surrounding him.

Throughout his speeches, Job fluctuates between lamenting his personal condition and lamenting the plight of humanity in general, especially the oppressed. Both elements are present in his initial lament in chapter three. He begins by cursing his personal situation, and then proceeds to bemoan the sad fate of all sufferers.

Job's final major speech in chapters 29-31 is essentially a lament of his fate in the form of a public self-testimony and examination of conscience. The manner in which Job tells his story and laments his fate is an excellent model for care-givers and sufferers. When confronted with great suffering and intense emotions, the healthiest response is simply to voice our lament and tell our story. If those around us imitate Job's friends in their unwillingness to listen, we can follow Job's example by gradually redirecting our complaints toward God. In God's twofold affirmation of Job's honesty in the epilogue,[11] we have assurance that God wants to hear what is on our mind and in our heart, and that he appreciates our candor.

A lament can be composed of a variety of emotions and dispositions, including the following found in Job: anguish (chapter 3), frustration and alienation (chapter 6), depression (chapter 7), anger (chapters 9-10), and defiance (chapter 31).

The lament is an intermediate stage of the coping process that can be a fruitful source of insights not only into one's own life, but into reality in general. The quality of a lament is determined by its sincerity and depth. What is most important in a lament is the honest expression of feelings, experiences, and internal images, and one's practical response to the lament either as a sufferer or care-giver. A lament can be a catalyst for good or evil, health or illness, growth or destruction.

Health and Growth Considerations

Constructive expression of emotions constitutes a healthy step in the process of feelings clarification. Feelings resolution generally occurs gradually, leaving various scars. One usually retains some painful memories of an unhappy event even when the acuity of the feelings has subsided. A good barometer of the healing process is whether one ceases to experience a physical stress response when the painful incident is recalled.

Science Amid Suffering: Lectures in Theology, Philosophy, and Morality

Popular faith and expression of emotions are at the level of belief and experience rather than theology. It is not until the friends enter the discussion that a more doctrinal and philosophical approach is taken. Their dogmatic, judgmental attitude leads to the breakdown of communications with Job, who gradually turns his attention from the friends and implores not only God but some vague heavenly advocate[12] who he hopes will secure his rights in court. Insensitive use of scientific or rational language in situations of suffering can squelch communication channels and alienate the sufferer. Not all sufferers will have the perseverance and integrity of Job which enabled him to confront God when his friends would no longer listen.

God-Talk

The monotonous, convoluted speeches of the friends vividly demonstrate that theology, the rational, scientific way of speaking about God, is usually an inappropriate pastoral response to human suffering. The exceptions to this are generally quite obvious, such as when sufferers exhibit a desire to talk about God or religious doctrine, perhaps to rid themselves of unhealthy religious beliefs that are exacerbating their pain. Untimely God-talk often originates from nervous, ill-at-ease care-givers who sincerely want to help the sufferer, but are struggling with their own emotions. Care-givers can also be influenced by bad theology and naiveté born of inexperience.

Job's friends were influenced both by retribution theology[13] and their own apparent unfamiliarity with dire situations of suffering. Their remarks reveal their ignorance or misinterpretation of the dynamics of the situation. Their inexperience in such matters takes the form of an endless litany of easy answers that sufferers of all eras have come to dread.

Common theological responses of God-talk are: "Well, I guess it was God's will...God knows what's best...He needs _____ more in heaven than on earth..."

Personal Philosophy

Philosophical statements are also generally inappropriate. They are opinions and speculation at a time when compassionate actions and love are required. Comforters often philosophize without realizing it. As with the theological response, it can be a nervous, well-intentioned reaction with unforeseen consequences or implications. The temptation to project our personal philosophy on those faced with difficult circumstances is both subtle and potent. As an alternative to such simplistic projection, we should consider the variables and ambiguities of their situation. Perhaps the choices and consequences facing them are more complicated than it appears. If our philosophy has any value for the sufferer, that person will usually indicate so, and we can then share it according to the individual's circumstances and needs.

The following are examples of inappropriate and potentially explosive philosophical statements in response to death: "Oh well, we all have to go sometime...I guess it must have been their time to go...Things always work out for the best..."

Morality

Moral judgments are especially untimely during suffering, not only because they may be incorrect, as in Job's case, but for the guilt they invite. The primary focus of the care-giver should be on comforting the sufferer rather than judging their morality. Moral issues have their place, but must be discussed according to the timing of the sufferer.[14]

Morality statements frequently contain the verb qualifiers "must," "should," and "ought to." The following are examples of morality statements: "Well, fast living tends to catch up to a person...God must have had some sort of message for you in this accident...You must have done something wrong in order to merit this...You should have known better..."

Suffering and Science: Mixing Apples and Oranges

The effectiveness of theological, philosophical, and morality statements will depend on how, to whom, and when they are spoken. The fact that they may be objectively true does not make them appropriate in every circumstance. Suffering always occurs in a personal and pastoral context. The disciplines of theology, philosophy, and morality are not designed to address specific cases of suffering as if they occur in a vacuum. They should be applied only at the conscious or subconscious initiative of the sufferer, such as when they show an apparent need or inclination to communicate on this level.

The care-giver's fundamental role is that of friend and listener rather than teacher. Frequently, the sufferer becomes the teacher and source of inspiration. Familiarity with the psycho-spiritual state and personal background of the sufferer will help the care-giver proceed sensitively and gently in their discussions. While listening is an indispensable element of each stage of the coping process, it is especially important in the context of theology, personal philosophies, and morality because of the deep hurts and misunderstandings that can be sustained by both sufferer and care-giver.

Justice and Disorientation[15]

As an outgrowth of the language of gut feelings and protest, the language of justice and disorientation refers to the crisis that sufferers experience when they discover that their neat and tidy conceptions of life and its fairness no longer hold.

Prior to chapter 21, Job had been pleading for an arbiter and eventually an avenger who would take his side before God. This plea reaches its summit in chapter 19 with Job expressing his hope of final vindication, while warning his friends that their callousness and unfounded judgments would not go unpunished.[16] In chapters 21, 23, and 24, Job's rebellion against God for what he perceives as unfair treatment expands to a consideration of the rampant injustices that exist in the world. In the stage of justice and disorientation, sufferers begin to question the very roots of their faith in light of the massive human suffering and the seemingly unpunished transgressions of the wicked which surround them. This discovery constitutes a direct contradiction of the retribution mentality which was so pervasive in Job's world, as it is in ours.

In chapter 23, Job expresses his disorientation in very poignant terms. His world has been turned upside down; he has sought God for vindication and support, yet he is unable to find him. Job truly knows what it is to ask where is God when you need him! In this disorientation, Job makes the painful, almost frightening discovery that human principles of retribution and justice do not adequately explain divine justice. Moral goodness is not always rewarded with prosperity, nor evil with misfortune. God seems to ignore the prayers of the wounded and dying, the very people who the law and prophets affirmed were objects of his special care.[17] Lacking an alternative life vision, all Job can do is affirm his own integrity, speak what he feels is the truth, and persist in his cause.

All explanations and justifications for his afflictions fail, but Job loses neither heart nor faith. He doesn't permit self-doubt or his crisis of faith to cause him to give up. It is not insignificant that although he prays for death, Job never contemplates suicide. This constitutes a priceless affirmation of God's sovereignty over life no matter what the circumstances.

Job believes in the depths of his being that both life and death must be placed in God's hands, but this does not induce him to shrink from being honest with God for fear of divine reprisal. Job believes that his own justice or integrity is worth dying for, and he is willing to pay the price. Such blind and dogged faith is sometimes the only refuge the sufferer has against apathy and despair.

Job's dreadful circumstances and utter helplessness have brought him to a stalemate position. All he can do is wait for God to respond to his situation. When suffering pushes us to the limit, it is only the mysterious interaction between divine providence and human cooperation that lends meaning to the present and offers hope in the future.

Mystery

The wisdom poem (chapter 28) interrupts the dialogue by replacing the language of theology with the language of mystery. It uses the literary forms of story and analogy to discuss a reality that defies description. While the language of mystery constitutes an improvement in accuracy and sensitivity over the rational sciences discussed above, it nonetheless dismisses rather than resolves the question of theodicy (i.e. the justice of God in light of human suffering). It is an impersonal solution to a personal problem.

When we suffer, we desire neither the simplistic answers of Job's friends nor philosophical non-answers such as the wisdom poem. Because suffering is a mystery, this mode of language is helpful for leading the sufferer to a more theologically correct understanding of their situation. However, it lacks the compassionate personal element necessary to humanize the healing process. It recognizes the paradoxical quality of a particular truth or reality without providing a human or divine channel for feedback and communication. We can infer Job's dissatisfaction with the wisdom poem from his continued speech and closing statements.[18]

Although profound and insightful, the language of mystery lacks the potency to move the sufferer to the point of personal acceptance. It offers no tangible hope, personal encounter, or relationship as an antidote to the individual's pain.

Recollection and Story

In chapters 29-31, Job gives a final self-testimony in the form of a public examination of conscience. Job emerges from his laments, provocative questions, and bold challenges to bare his soul to the world. In his moving words, we discover perhaps the most human of all the stages of suffering, which we entitle recollection and story.

Job ventures back into his personal history to claim and share his story. He recalls in vivid detail the joys and lifestyle which he has experienced. Unlike the sentimental portrayals of such reminiscing often found in modern films and literature, Job's recollection has a moral and spiritual tone to supplement the emotional and historical. Job's affirmation of his integrity in 29:12-20 and chapter 31 is more than a sentimental recounting of past activities; it is the fruit of deep soul-searching that compels him to bear his soul before God and his friends. Interwoven with Job's past exploits is a moving and graphic tale of his present tragedy.[19] Job needs to tell all, both the good and the bad, past and present, including his fears about the future.

Although Job's friends' thoughts are not revealed, I believe their silence[20] is significant. At the beginning of their dialogue they couldn't resist the urge to respond to Job's laments and scandalous accusations of God and religious orthodoxy; now they remain silent in response to his tragic tale. Perhaps Job appealed to the sense of fidelity and compassion which had compelled them to visit and mourn with him in the first place. They could refute his accusations and observations, but they were helpless before his tender life story. Their silence constitutes a lesson for both sufferers and care-givers that can be summed up as follows: Sufferers, tell your story, both to God and trusted confidants. Enter more deeply into your past, present, and apprehension about the future. Confront your pain to the degree you can bear, and share it with others, especially God. Apparently, Job's story hit a nerve with God, who perhaps couldn't resist manifesting compassion, reassurance, and cosmic marvels to Job in a personal way. For care-givers, the message seems to be: Listen, be present in mind, body, and spirit, and learn the value of timely silence and waiting on the Lord. Encourage the sufferers to tell their story, so that both sufferers and care-givers can learn from these sensitive revelations.

Such recollection and story-telling is both painful and cathartic. It is a step in the direction of healing and transformation rather than simply a band-aid or relief. The Bible is an immense compendium of recollected events and stories within stories that speak of the joys, pains, fears, and hopes of the human race. Stories do not give answers so much as they provide a path and inspiration for living with mysteries beyond human comprehension. When we read Job or indeed any of the Bible using *lectio divina,* we are simply reading their story in light of ours, and listening for the light God's word sheds not only on their circumstances, but on ours. The stories in the Bible are existential in nature: they are properly understood not only as past events, but as present realities which call the believer to certain attitudes, beliefs, and behaviors. This is how the ancients understood the Bible, and why they clung to God's word despite many trials and hardships. It was not just a word spoken to their ancestors; it was a message meant for them as well.

In telling his story, Job reveals that he has lost some of his confidence in God's special providence and initiative in both his own life and in the world at large. In the prologue, Job could assert piously that God both gave and took away, and his name should be blessed. During the dialogue, God gradually becomes a remote and foreign deity whose activity Job no longer comprehends or even recognizes. Job, like us, stands in need of God's mysterious and gracious self-revelation.

God's revelation to Job out of the whirlwind[21] occurred in God's own time, and Job was disposed to receive it. He had spoken his piece, and was waiting expectantly for the Lord. He had doubts and insecurities just as we do, but he took the risk of hoping and trusting in God. Job did not arrive at this receptive state of contemplation through some innate mystical gift or experience. It was hard work, perseverance, and risk-taking honesty that kept Job's heart open to hear God's word when it finally came.

True to human experience, there will be an interlude between Job's final testimony and his contemplative encounter (or God's mysterious revelation, from whichever perspective you choose to view it). God works through and despite human actions and events. While Job's old friends had retreated into silence in the face of Job's story and stubborn pleas of innocence, a new friend surfaces in chapter 32 who we might say is representative of "the new theology." His answers are better, but still don't suffice, at least for Job. There are elements of Elihu in all of us who have looked deeply into profound questions and arrived at answers and coping mechanisms with which we are comfortable. The challenge for care-givers is to share the fruits of our labors without disheveling the soil of others. Through Elihu's unrestrained enthusiasm, we can learn that sharing gifts is one thing, but presuming their acceptance by others is quite another.

Charismatic Prophecy[22]

As Job and his friends conclude their dialogue, an enthusiastic young theologian, whose presence had not been disclosed previously, speaks up. Armed with bold insights and a specific agenda, Elihu rebukes both Job and his friends for their weak theology and inconclusive arguments. In fairness to Elihu, his theology is more refined than that of Job's older friends, and does foreshadow elements of the Yahweh speeches to follow. Although he primarily speaks the language of theology, Elihu

does incorporate elements of contemplation drawn from his observance of the natural order. We speak of Elihu as a charismatic prophet based on his anticipation of the contemplative dimension of the Yahweh speeches. He offers sound advice to Job and all sufferers concerning the majesty of God, the testimony of nature, and the humble state of humanity before God. Despite these insights, Elihu's message is impaired by his precocious and judgmental attitude. Even the gift of prophecy (i.e. speaking in the name of God) can be marred by presumption and a retributive outlook.

The language of charismatic prophecy is present whenever persons claim to speak in the name of God. Because we are dealing with the gifts of the Spirit, credence must be given to this form of language as a medium for expressing compassion. It is obviously difficult to determine the validity of these claims, and therefore one must emulate the church in approaching these situations with caution.

Charismatic prophecy need not be explicit and self-proclaimed. Actions and words can be anonymously prophetic; they can reveal God's will and presence without drawing attention to their supernatural origins.[23] Used in accordance with God's will, prophetic language bears the fruits of love, compassion, repentance, and healing. Conversely, when it is tainted by opportunism or insensitive application, it can do extensive psycho-spiritual harm to individuals.

While authentic charismatic prophecy is an important therapeutic tool, it remains a second-hand method of coping. The response from God is mediated and thus bears somewhat of an impersonal tone. It was not good enough for Job,[24] nor need it be sufficient for us. When you want God badly enough, you'll dial direct and accept the consequences. While third parties can help you make the connection, they remain only the preface or background to the desired communication. No one who experiences the next form of coping language would call it impersonal or indirect.

Contemplation

The language of contemplation is a natural extension of the language of mystery, for it places mystery in the context of the basic human relationships (i.e. with God, self, others, and the material world). The consecration of our hearts and spirit to God is a healthy complement to the language of mystery, which can tend to stay at the level of head knowledge. In contemplation, we humbly and receptively place ourselves before the mystery and presence of God. Contemplation expands the horizon of the sufferer by introducing the possibility of a new and different perception of and response to their situation. Contemplative language is designed to distract individuals' attention from themselves and toward an object currently more deserving of their attention.

The Yahweh speeches draw Job into contemplation by diverting his attention from himself and toward God's mysterious presence in the world. In the natural self-absorption which consumed Job amid his afflictions, his attention had been diverted only to recognize the prevalence of wickedness in the world and the failure of divine justice from a human justice standpoint. Now Yahweh invites Job to examine aspects of God's involvement with nature, the wicked, and the forces of chaos that had previously escaped him. He invites Job to experience his suffering from a theocentric (God-centered) perspective on life. In discovering that his own world view was sadly deficient, Job is liberated by the vision born of contemplation. He can now make the transition from an anthropocentric (humanity-centered) world view to a theocentric perspective. While this does not take away the pain, it enables the sufferer to find meaning even in the most tragic of circumstances.

Fundamental to the theocentric perspective is the principle that the will of God ultimately takes precedence over even legitimate human needs. This is the fundamental goal and challenge of not only contemplation, but the whole Judeo-Christian spiritual life. While from a secular humanist's perspective this might seem absurd, what consolation can secular humanism offer to individuals and families stricken by inexplicable tragedy? Is there any consolation that will suffice short of that which comes from faith and experience of God?

Contemplation is a path for encountering and coping with the related mysteries of providence, divine justice, and human suffering. Yahweh's revelation of his providence for the animal kingdom and his ordering of the cycles of nature are colorful examples of contemplative language. They seek to draw the listener into a transformed understanding of the object of attention. Contemplative language seeks to understand things from a different perspective, and thereby create or affirm a vision that enables the individual to cope with and transcend their particular affliction.

It is no accident that contemplation constitutes the final step in the process of *lectio divina*.[25] The reader who holistically encounters persons, events, and teachings in the Bible is invited to go beyond their anthropocentric framework and experience God as the underlying and fundamental reality of the universe. In the final chapter, we will discuss how *lectio divina* may be appropriate in certain care-giving situations as a framework for helping individuals find meaning, motivation, and hope amid their suffering.

Practical Considerations

● Like Job, most sufferers are able to enter the world of contemplation only after enduring several of the previous stages. The preceding stages of language are placed in the proper perspective and context through contemplation. For example, popular faith or theological statements (classification depending on the situation and faith level of the individual) such as "The Lord gave and the Lord has taken away; blessed be the name of the Lord" are excellent subjects for contemplation. They contain numerous levels of meaning and offer an inexhaustible source for reflection. As our experience of God and life evolves and deepens, these declarations of faith and praise can take on different meanings each time we encounter them. Elements of mystery (e.g. nature) or gut-level emotional expression (an outburst or lament) may also be suitable for contemplation. In the case of an outburst or lament, we might sit in silence before God and ask him to help us discover an underlying message or moral. What does our behavior tell us about our personality, situation, lifestyle, etc.?

● Because the language of contemplation is designed to induce a surrender to the divine, it is incompatible with rigid, self-willed objectives. Since the experience of contemplation varies with the individual, it is non-competitive and not amenable to precise analysis. The best barometer of the quality of the believers' contemplative experience is the fruit that becomes evident in their life.

● Contemplation brings the language of silence to its completion. The soul rests in God, who transcends all forms of language and expression.

● A frequent consequence of contemplation is the realization that our response to suffering is misguided and in need of some change in attitude or action. For example, we may have dwelled on the deprivation of some gift without considering the positive aspects of the situation. Through contemplation, we could discover that a particular attitude or behavior pattern is impeding the coping and healing process. Contemplation may lead us to simplify or modify some aspect of our behavior or lifestyle, thereby reducing or eliminating certain sources of stress, and facilitating a more harmonious experience of life.

The Contemplative Dimension of Care-Giving

If contemplation is the sufferer's path to God and healing, we must ask how as care-givers we can facilitate this journey for others. For care-givers untrained in spiritual direction and counseling, it is easier to answer this question in the negative than the positive. Contemplation is a potentially complex element of the spiritual life that is best practiced and discerned with the aid of a support group or trained spiritual director. Further, because faith traditions have distinct perspectives on suffering and contemplation, a good general approach for care-givers is to ask: How can I keep my ego and agenda out of the sufferer's healing and spiritual growth process while doing little things to show support and solidarity?

Job's friends give an excellent example of things you don't do: Lecture, interrupt, listen poorly, judge, accuse, rationalize, theologize, philosophize, moralize, oversimplify, argue, and project personal insecurities onto the sufferer. The friends' preference of theology and judgment over prayer, mercy, and compassion was the seed of their downfall. They believed that their mastery of tradition entitled them to act as spokesmen for God. This presumption unconsciously inhibited their capacity to listen.

From afar, these errors seem simple to avoid. However, they become quite a temptation when you are emotionally involved in the suffering of a loved one or someone you serve as a professional or volunteer. Contemplation helps us stay attuned to the needs of the sufferer while monitoring our tendency to project our inner conflicts and weaknesses into the care-giving encounter.

Contemplation Begins at Home

We are likely to imitate Job's friends unless we integrate contemplation into our care-giving efforts. Contemplation and compassion are interdependent. To function properly, both must be present. Both point to God as their source. How can we mediate God's love, mercy, and presence to others if we don't know him through prayer and contemplation? How can we claim to know and communicate with God if we refuse to be with others in their pain? Linguistically, compassion is presence to someone amidst suffering. Both in suffering and care-giving, head knowledge (theology) is no substitute for heart knowledge (faith). If we gradually cultivate a contemplative dimension in our care-giving, we will be less vulnerable to our personal weaknesses and the temptations of insensitivity and presumption.

We are quite misled if we think we can help others deal

with their pain when we are unwilling to confront our own. We must be in touch with our own experience of suffering. Without at least a basic awareness of our own pain, we will inevitably project onto others the therapies that may or may not work for us. As care-givers, we journey with the sufferer in discovering mutually acceptable and therapeutic ways of speaking to and about God during suffering.

Contemplation and Elitism

We must be wary of understanding contemplation in an exclusive, possessive manner. Contemplation is not a privileged mystical experience available only to those advanced in the spiritual life. God offers the gift of contemplation, of seeing things rightly and experiencing the divine, to all persons. It is not for us to make judgments as to different degrees of contemplation or whether one person's experience or practice is superior to another's. God and the fruits manifested in our actions are the only judges of the efficacy of our contemplation.

We must keep in mind that contemplation is ultimately the mysterious interaction of God and the individual. We can promote contemplation through word, deed, and disposition, but the choice ultimately lies with the individual. We are simply the Lord's servants at the disposal of both God and our fellow person. We will defeat our purposes if we take ourselves too seriously or perceive the work of healing as primarily ours rather than God's.

Resources on Contemplation

The contemplation we have been speaking of includes both silent, receptive presence before God, and an active awareness of God's presence in creation, human events, and human beings. Although contemplation is simple in theory and practice, the psycho-spiritual issues and experiences that arise as one practices it go beyond the scope of this book. Further, brief instruction might portray contemplation in a mechanical or methodical fashion that would categorize the movement of the Spirit.

Contemplation is a mysterious interaction between God and humanity sustained by grace and human cooperation that must remain free of rigid human frameworks, expectations, and constraints. The proper context for instruction on contemplation is books, private instruction and counseling, courses, and workshops on prayer, *lectio divina,* and spirituality. Most spiritual guides recommend a moderate amount of informational reading. Individuals usually prefer to have some theological and practical instruction on contemplation as a supplement to their daily prayers and experiences. Too much reading presents the danger of making contemplation a primarily intellectual activity rather than a holistic affair of the head, senses, and heart. Because books on the aforementioned topics can appear daunting to beginners, and boring to experienced contemplatives, with several exceptions I will defer my recommendations to the Suggestions for Further Reading.

I have found Cardinal Carlo Martini, S.J.'s *Praying with St. Luke* to be the most readable and practical book on Christian prayer and contemplation in the context of *lectio divina.* A Jewish author on prayer and spirituality whom many have found to be insightful is Rabbi Abraham Joshua Heschel. Works by Thomas Keating, Thomas Merton, Thomas Shannon, and Thomas Green are also highly recommended.

Reconciliation

Just as the Yahweh speeches[26] and Job's acceptance speech,[27] despite their profundity, are only the prelude to the resolution of the story, so the language of contemplation is not the final word in regard to suffering. The narrator of Job deftly communicates this in the epilogue through two comments. First, Yahweh makes the retribution-minded friends dependent on the intercession of Job. Second, Job's fortunes are restored twofold after he intercedes for his friends. Contemplation is empty and vain without the guts of the spiritual journey, which is love.[28] Reconciliation is love in action.

Culmination of the Spiritual Journey

For the author of Job, the proof is in the pudding. As magnificent as Job's contemplative experience was, it is useless unless manifested in a corresponding transformation of attitude and action. Job's need for a more reconciliatory disposition was revealed at various points in the dialogue. He was weaned on and influenced by retribution doctrine just as the friends were. An example of his retributive attitude is his warning to the friends in 19:28-29: "But you who say, 'How shall we persecute him, seeing that the root of the matter is found in him?' be afraid of the sword for yourselves, for these crimes deserve the sword; that you may know that there is a judgment." A transformation of consciousness was necessary for Job to pass over from retribution to reconciliation.

Although all the stages of coping language discussed so far had their place in Job's maturation process, it was the contemplative encounter that catalyzed his journey toward reconciliation with God. Contemplation is the stepping stone rather than the summit of wholeness and holiness. Just as the contemplative encounter was consummated in Job's personal confession of faith,[29] so his new perspective on life must be consummated in the act of reconciliation, the direct antithesis of retribution. The author of Job has demonstrated the inadequacies of retribution doctrine, and has offered an alternative life vision based on reconciliation and gratuitous love.

Reconciliation: Love in Action

The language of reconciliation is a practical language of unconditional love that derives its strength from intimacy with the divine. It is composed of words and images of compassion, mercy, and forgiveness, as well as non-verbal modes such as touching, smiling, and listening. It is expressed in practical circumstances and is keenly aware of human weaknesses and limitations. For Christians, the ultimate manifestation of the language of reconciliation occurs on Calvary[30] under conditions worse than Job's.

The language of reconciliation provides the answer to the critical questions posed by Job and Yahweh. In response to God's initiative, Job must reconcile with God, his situation, and even his stubborn friends. God gave Job no straightforward answers to inspire this reconciliation; rather, he invited Job to look beyond the imperfections inherent in all relationships, and discover the fundamental beauty and wonder in all aspects of life. Reconciliation is not the language of self-interest, certainty, and security, but of humility, acceptance, and trust. It is the most practical of languages, for it always occurs in the context of a relationship. When we suffer, we may need to reconcile ourselves on a number of levels: with nature or the material world, other persons, God, or our situation.

The Joban call to unconditional love and service is the meeting place of religion, suffering, care-giving, friendship, and human potential. Through grace, the hard questions and violent struggles of suffering and care-giving culminate in the transformational and redemptive power of compassion and reconciliation. Without trust and personal integrity, two qualities for which Job is rightly famous, the possibilities for inner healing, reconciliation, and true friendship are quite limited. In the next chapter, we will look at both positive and negative examples of trust and integrity in the book of Job with an eye to applications for the care-giver in a world increasingly devoid of these values.

Reflection Questions

Practical Experiences of Job's Language of Suffering and Care-Giving

How has your experience as a care-giver mirrored any or all of these stages?

How might consciousness of these stages be helpful to you in your care-giving efforts? Would they influence the way you respond to sufferers in a given situation? If so, how?

Personal Applications

What has been your experience of these stages during times of personal suffering? Compare your reaction with Job's, noting both similarities and differences.

How might awareness of these stages be personally helpful to you? What therapeutic or comforting attitudes or actions could they inspire in certain situations?

How do you feel about contemplation? If you are interested in practicing it in a deeper way, how might you go about this?

What are some impediments to contemplation in your life?

Do you have a reconciliatory disposition? How do you feel about reconciliation? Do any memories, attitudes, or hurts hold you back from it? What personal experiences, events, or relationships come to mind?

CHAPTER FIVE

Trust and Integrity:
Essential Care-Giver Dispositions

One of the lessons of Job for care-givers is the importance of trust and integrity. These values are central to our relationships with God, others, and ourselves. Modern society's preoccupation with self has resulted in a gradual de-emphasis of these values. Such self-absorption gradually leads to a distortion of all our relationships, including the self-image. In this chapter, we will reflect upon how the contrasting dispositions of the four principal characters in Job can inspire us to build the foundation of our vocation, religion, human relationships, and self-image on these sturdy values.

Mrs. Job

Mrs. Job can be viewed as a realistic model of both sufferer and care-giver reaction to tragedy. Mrs. Job acts as care-giver in response to Job's physical afflictions, while she shares in his suffering the loss of children and fortune. She teaches us the reality of hopelessness and despair. Her words to Job in verse 2:9 indicate that she no longer trusts God, and therefore holding on to one's integrity is not a credible alternative. She does not possess the level of trust and integrity necessary to endure such tragic events. The text is noticeably silent on her future disposition; we do not know whether she repents or falls deeper into despair. From a health perspective, we should note that Mrs. Job did not repress her feelings. This makes it easier in the long term on both herself and her care-givers. At least everyone knows where she stands, and approximately what she is feeling. It is easier for care-givers to deal with someone whose disposition is obvious rather than with an individual who retreats inward and represses intense emotions.

Although her brief appearance in Job and the author's silence on her innermost feelings leave the interpretation of her character to the reader, we would be mistaken if we impulsively adopt a judgmental attitude toward her. Before we criticize her, we must ask ourselves whether we would waver in the face of such overwhelming circumstances. There is a part in each of us that is Mrs. Job; in the face of certain trials, we could lose heart and at least temporarily reject the beliefs and values that have guided us throughout our lives. We could become rebellious and defiant in the face of human tragedy.

We know from the Bible that God is not stoic or casual concerning human misfortunes, nor should we be. The critical question for both Mrs. Job and us is: What will we do with our anger? Will we channel it constructively or let it destroy us and others? Mrs. Job serves as a caution against judging those who yield to despair. Note that Job rebukes and corrects his wife; he does not judge or condemn her. His prudence and moderation set an inspired example for care-givers who meet individuals in the mold of Mrs. Job. It is only through grace (in unison with human cooperation), as demonstrated in God's reconciliation-inspiring revelation to Job, that we can endure such ultimate tests.

The brief verbal exchange between Job and Mrs. Job dramatizes the decisive choice that both sufferers and care-givers face in response to misfortune. Faithfulness and perseverance is a difficult path that requires communication and cooperation between God and humanity.

Job's Friends

Job's friends, whose attitudes and dispositions appear similar enough to be considered together as one character, display a striking lack of integrity and trust. They give us the impression that they trust neither themselves, God, nor others. They exemplify the part of ourselves that is insecure, fearful, and defensive. They project their lack of self-trust onto both God and Job, and disguise it with religious zeal. Were it not for this profound lack of trust in themselves and God, it seems doubtful they would have assaulted Job so persistently.

Their lack of integrity is primarily a consequence of immaturity and superficiality. They seem to have been relatively sheltered from innocent suffering, or perhaps they have simply closed their eyes to it. In any case, if we define integrity as holistic commitment to a core set of values, we can state that while they are committed to the values of their retribution-based theological tradition, they have not considered its full ramifications. Because of their naiveté and lack of compassion, these purported wise men who present themselves as persons of integrity turn out to be otherwise.

The friends exemplify the part of ourselves that is unwilling to go deeper, that is complacent in the present, that uses moral, philosophical, or religious beliefs as a cloak for fear, inner dishonesty, and a judgmental attitude. They lack a certain wholeness and consistency that can be gained only through suffering and experience. Their unwillingness to enter more deeply into Job's suffering keeps them at a distance from God even though they claim to be his spokesmen.

As care-givers, we may encounter individuals who remind us of Job's friends. We may see the friends in religious individuals who self-righteously chide a suffering friend or family member for committing a certain act or sin which apparently results in their affliction. In the manner of Job's friends, they become an accuser of the sufferer.

In Job's debate with his self-assured counselors, it eventually becomes apparent that rational arguments are of no avail. Only a divine rebuke can dislodge Job's friends from their intransigence. When used in a timely and natural manner, silence and humor[31] can help disarm such combative individuals. We can usually assume that such a pious exterior hides a profound lack of self-esteem and trust in God. They are not what they seem, and require the most delicate handling.

We cannot fight the battle on their turf; we must move them gently to a space where they feel less compelled to put up a front and resort to familiar defensive tactics. If we feel a need to confront them, this must be done gently and privately. Any suggestions or corrections must be cushioned with positive affirmation and sincere caring. We must avoid any words or gestures that hint of condescension or destructive criticism. We should also be prepared for an initial rebuff or reprisal. Like Job, we must forgive and intercede for them, rather than judge them.

Job

Job is a person of integrity and trust. Having been described as a person of integrity by God in both the prologue and epilogue,[32] he is a model of human wholeness. Such wholeness does not imply a life without conflicts, doubts, insecurities, or troublesome passions and emotions; rather, it implies a commitment to a core set of beliefs and values that are worth living and dying for. Job was ready to confront God even though he believed it might cost him his life.[33]

In his willingness to challenge God, Job reveals a deep sense of trust, love, and respect for God. Job could have said to himself: "Why bother with this so-called God? I know that I have done nothing to merit this degree of suffering, yet he is silent and refuses to deliver me. Apparently my religious beliefs were wrong and I should simply give up the faith, for if this is where it leads, it is not worth retaining anyway."

We are indebted to Job for revealing the true nature of trust and integrity. Ironically, he is an exact inverse of the friends. They portray themselves as trustworthy persons of integrity when in reality their lack of self-knowledge and immature faith causes them to be accusers of Job and witnesses against God. They are the opposite of what they appear. Conversely, Job, whose skin disease would have been interpreted by his culture as a sure sign of God's disapproval and wrath, is in reality a witness to both God and the truth. This person whose wild, nearly blasphemous words would seem to indicate that he has absolutely no trust in God is revealed to be a person who speaks truthfully, i.e. with integrity. The trustworthiness of Job is also revealed by God. In the prologue, he trusted Job to withstand the excruciating tests wrought by Satan; in the epilogue, he trusted Job to obey him and intercede for his friends.

Just as we can resemble Mrs. Job and Job's friends, we also have the heart of Job in us. There are elements of Job in each of us, not only in our experience of innocent suffering, but in our potential to hold out and be true to ourselves and God. This is not a natural ability independent of God's grace. Rather, it is a gift that is activated through a combination of human effort and God's mysterious providence and initiative, which often manifests itself, as in Job's case, when we least expect it.

Job is also an excellent model of self-esteem. Despite overwhelming physical, emotional, and spiritual evidence to the contrary, Job continues to believe in himself. He knows he isn't perfect,[34] but nonetheless deserves respect and fair treatment. We can imagine Job saying to himself (and to us as well): "I am made in the image of God, little lower than the angels, and I am worth something, at least in God's eyes and in mine if in no one else's. I don't understand why he has permitted my unjust and dreadful circumstances. Even though in the back of my mind there is concern that God is angry with me, I will continue to go with my gut feelings and hope in him while believing in myself. I don't care how long my friends and family question my integrity; I will continue to hold it fast."

Verses 27:2-6 of Job eloquently express Job's passion for truth and his own dignity/integrity: "As God lives, who withholds my deserts, the Almighty, who has made bitter my soul, so long as I still have life in me and the breath of God is in my nostrils, my lips shall not speak falsehood, nor my tongue utter deceit! Far be it from me to account you right; till I die I will not renounce my innocence. My justice I maintain and I will not relinquish it; my heart does not reproach me for any of my days."

Energized by his commitment to both God's integrity and his own, Job stands as the patriarch and model of motivation. Job is not motivated by possessions, power, or status. Rather, he is motivated by self-respect which we can presume to be both healthy and exaggerated. While it is good that Job believes so strongly in himself, he oversteps his bounds when he asserts that his integrity places him on a level from which he can hold God accountable in the matter of justice and judgment. God uses Job's suffering as an opportunity to expose and modify this exaggerated sense of self. If a whole person such as Job has need of discipline and correction, can we presume that we will be different? Such acknowledgment of human frailty and divine confidence manifested in correction is especially liberating during troubled times.

In the midst of suffering, we see ourselves in Job who felt entitled to humane treatment by God and his friends. The friends may not have respected his claim, but God did. God's respect for Job's dignity does not inhibit his freedom to act in ways contrary to Job's wishes, though ultimately in his best interests. Job had to reflect, pray, persevere, and contemplate so that he could rediscover God's presence and friendship. When we feel abandoned either personally or in our vocation, we can recall the witness and testimony of Job, and tenaciously hold on to our integrity and hope.

Job is a model for the care-giver both in his trust in God and in God's trust in him. Job is the type of person in whom we can place our confidence, and to whom we can reveal those intimate and painful parts of ourselves which need healing. Job is that part of ourselves which can be available and present to others, and which respects others' vulnerabilities because we are profoundly aware of our own. Unlike the friends, who know neither reality nor themselves in the deepest sense, Job is symbolic of the human ability and vocation to accept reality and ourselves in both the painful and the joyful aspects of life. In this disposition, we reveal a gut-level trust in God, for we could not face our problems unless we felt we had someone behind us who was able to help us in our weakness. Because we do not deny or flee the dark side of human existence, we are able to appreciate the light side more. We gradually become contemplative care-givers who in their sincere presence to persons in pain invite trust, hope, and confidence.

God

One of the most difficult aspects of suffering is the challenge to retain trust in God when we feel abandoned by both God and humanity. Because this is always easier to preach than to put into practice, we will limit ourselves to stating that Job is a book that extols the power of prayer and perseverance. It gives no material guarantees and reassures us only in the language of faith. We are told not that we will always like our reality, but that God is present, active, and has a mysterious and incomprehensible plan and design for each of us, as well as for the rest of creation. The testing of Job as paralleled in the testing we experience indicates not only that God has confidence in each of us, but that the response he wills for us fits into his overall plan and providence for creation. The wrench in the works is that we often exercise our freedom to say no to God's will and plan. This ultimately results in humanity's mistrust of God, fellow persons, creation, and the self. Because utopian platitudes and naive resolutions will not stand up in the suspicious, broken world we live in, we must turn continually to prayer, contemplation, and meditation on God's word as a path for rediscovering God's integrity and presence as well as our own integrity and trustworthiness.

The Path of Trust and Reconciliation

The profound message of Job is that our trust in God must be based on his terms and world-view rather than ours. It is God's will, not ours, that is of greatest importance. This is fine in theory, but difficult in practice. God's will, whether direct or permissive, becomes hard to swallow, even scandalous, when we experience severe suffering or minister to others in their pain. The integrity (or wholeness, justice) of God is not an empirical fact that can be proved or disproved, but a mystery that can be entered into through prayer, contemplation, and service. Our gradual discovery of the integrity of God will be paralleled by greater awareness of both our weaknesses and our strengths. The more fully we know ourselves, the more gentle we will be with peers, sufferers, and ourselves, for we will recognize that it is not innate virtue or perfection but the willingness to work toward forgiveness and reconciliation that is the primary manifestation of integrity and wholeness.

Following the example of God's playful response to Job,[35] we need to inject humor into our intense personal and professional lives. If we take ourselves or our vocation too seriously, as if everything depends on us, we risk becoming like Job's friends. If we become obsessive in our religious observance, we might remake God in our own image, a reflection of our desires and prejudices. If God would reveal the wonder and mysteries of creation to Job, he certainly will share these with us in his own time and way. It will be much easier to be disposed to his revelation if we have a sense of humor about ourselves and are not too self-absorbed. Humor lightens our load and dispenses of the baggage that gets in the way of our human and spiritual growth.

Job made it hard on himself by taking his integrity so seriously that he imagined himself a prince before God.[36] The transformed Job who was overwhelmed by the magnificence of God and creation[37] would probably be the first to advise us to let go of all pretentiousness and retain a certain humor about ourselves. While suffering is no laughing matter, life is at times. Given the craziness that goes on in the world today, care-givers must develop a sense of humor if only to preserve their sanity and enthusiasm. In the next chapter, we will integrate comments on the use of humor in care-giving with examples of the author of Job's presumed use of humor.

Reflection Questions

Trusting Oneself

In general, do you like and trust yourself? Consider why or why not.

Are there parts of yourself that you particularly like and trust, or dislike and mistrust? Why or why not?

Where did you learn both your trust and mistrust of self?

Trusting Others

Do you generally trust others? How is your disposition revealed in daily life? Consider some practical examples.

What keeps you from trusting others more? Have childhood, adolescent, or adult experiences discouraged you consciously or subconsciously from trusting others?

How does one distinguish trust from naiveté? What role do common sense and prudence play?

Trusting God

Do you trust God? Why or why not? What experiences have played a crucial role in forming your current disposition?

How do you feel God looks upon you? Is he pleased, disappointed, or somewhere in between?

Integrity

How would you define integrity?

How is integrity revealed in practical situations in your life?

What role does integrity play in your relationships with yourself, others, God, and the rest of creation? Consider some practical examples.

Do you believe integrity to be something difficult to achieve and rare to find in today's world? Why or why not?

What sacrifices and struggles might one expect to undergo in the process of living and working with integrity?

What Role(s) Do I Play?

With respect to the virtues of trust and integrity, do you see yourself in the characters in Job?

CHAPTER SIX

The Healing
Possibilities of Humor

Preface

In order to avoid being weighed down by the intensity or gravity of our vocation, we will need to discover daily opportunities for humor. Constructive humor is a healthy and refreshing component of everyday spirituality. Humor derives its potency from our reflections on the mysteries and paradoxes of life. It is important that we recognize opportunities for humor not only in Job, but in all of life. If we are going to suffer or care for those in pain, we would be wise to awaken ourselves to the humorous side of life.

When we speak of humor amid suffering, it is understood that it is a highly personal matter. Suffering can give rise to humor only at the sufferer's initiative. Care-givers and bystanders have no right to impose humor on someone in pain. As an aspect of holistic care-giving, humor is appropriate only when it heals or comforts. When humor is understood as a gift of God to refresh the mind, body, and spirit, and promote harmony and reconciliation, it becomes a moderating and therapeutic ingredient in the healing process. When we suffer, an ounce of humor is worth a ton of theology. We communicate compassion as much through smiles, touch, and tears as through words.

Humor for Care-Givers

Humor is important for both care-givers and sufferers. We know that care-giving as a vocation ranks among the highest in stress-related disorders. In almost every field within care-giving there is a personnel and resource shortage that makes for uncertainty and pressure. Sometimes it seems as if our care-giving efforts are largely futile, that both superiors and subordinates have no idea of our dilemma, or are unwilling to do what is necessary to improve circumstances; we then feel alienated and discouraged.

Family and everyday care-givers come up against similar constraints. There often doesn't seem to be enough time, energy, and material resources to meet the needs of ourselves and those we love. Humor is especially crucial when there is little we can do about our circumstances other than maintain a positive attitude. One thing harsh persons or circumstances cannot take away is the will to discover humor in situations. Recall the witticism (paraphrased) of St. Lawrence as he was being barbecued to death: "You can turn me over now. I'm done on this side."

Most people enjoy being around humorous people. The last thing sufferers and their family and friends need is another gloomy face. Sincere and natural efforts to cheer folks up may be one element of what the doctor ordered. People can tell forced or artificial humor. Unless humor is rooted deeply in our own disposition, it will not seem natural when we share it with others. Let's define what we mean by humor.

Humor is the ability to be enthused and amused by life, and to share this with others. Humor doesn't always make us laugh or smile, but it does lighten and relax our mind, body, and spirit. This is especially critical today with so many of us weighed down by physical, emotional, and spiritual burdens. Humor is fundamentally the fruit of a pliant, free spirit rather than a sharp wit or a quick mind, although these attributes can be humorous as well. Gestures, comments, and actions subtly designed to embarrass or harm others are not humor; they reflect insensitivity and cruelty.

The natural capacity for humor that we all possess requires development through practice and reflection. Humor is a natural component of prayer and contemplation, for it is certainly a gift from God—witness its potential to heal, reconcile, and renew.

A humorous person seeks to integrate the serious and sad elements of events, situations, and persons with their humorous aspects. Sometimes persons whom we would not normally regard as humorous have the most refined sense of humor. For example, read some of Mother Teresa's writings as well as writings about her that portray her as a human being and not just as a living saint. I don't think she or any other persons in her position could continue very long in their vocation if they didn't have a healthy dose of playfulness, humility, and irony in their approach to life. They know that as care-givers they are only instruments in the hands of God. The whole world isn't on their shoulders. When they make mistakes, they say they're sorry to God and the offended person, make reparation if possible, and then move on. When others offend them, they try to forgive and intercede for them.

It is quite fitting to give humor an inspired context, for where does it originate if not with God? The book of Job provides us with several examples of reconciliation and humor in the various relationships Job experiences.

The Comedy of Tragedy (Gallows Humor)

Job's tragedies, like ours, are not humorous in nature, yet they contain an element of irony that can evoke either laughter or tears. There can be a slim line between tragedy and comedy. In literary circles, Job is frequently referred to as a tragic comedy. It colorfully captures the unpredictable, paradoxical, and sometimes absurd nature of human existence.

We should not miss the opportunity to depart from seriousness for a few minutes to laugh (and perhaps cry as well) at life and ourselves when we discover Job-like experiences in our lives. Although the laughter may be colored with pain, it beats getting depressed. If we can't do anything about our situation, it is better to pray and find humor in it than to deny or fight it. As readers become more familiar with Job, they may encounter remarks and images that draw upon their experience and imagination, and give rise to humor and irony.

Humor, Paradox, and Imagination

A story about an individual who loses his entire fortune, family, and health in a matter of moments is hardly a typical setting for humor. If there is humor in Job, it must be dark humor, for the context is anything but funny. In literary comedy and tragedy, contradictions between expectations and reality evoke human laughter. Because Job's situation taken at face value is not funny, we will have to use our imagination.

Readers may initially object to this approach because it seems to depart from the literal meaning of the text. However, the many levels of meaning in Job and the obscurity of the Hebrew text make it contradictory to approach Job with a dogmatic "this is what it means" attitude. Because we know nothing biographical about the author nor do we knowingly possess any other texts written by him, we cannot presume to know the degree to which humor was an important aspect of his intent. Yet, the story is so filled with irony and exaggeration that we have as good a basis for projecting a sense of humor into the text as we do for denying it.

We must further note that our inquiry is in line with modern biblical studies. Principles of hermeneutics (the science of interpretation) applied to both secular and sacred texts affirm the validity of both the literal meaning of the text (what the author intended) and the applied meaning of the text (what it means to the reader). Further, the distinction between the two is not always clear.

Because we interpret a text based on our unique perspective and experience, there is always subjectivity. The objective/

literal and the subjective/applied meaning are both distinct and intertwined. To arrive at a balanced and practical interpretation of a text, the two must be kept in tension. The objective meaning bereft of the subjective becomes dry, impractical, and impersonal. The subjective meaning isolated from the objective is susceptible to biased projection, manipulation, and arbitrariness.

Several statements and developments in the text seem to include both a serious and humorous element, especially when we invoke our imagination. Such creativity is foreign neither to the author of Job nor to the Hebrew mind. The author's use of imagination is illustrated most graphically in the colorful Yahweh speeches, particularly Yahweh's descriptions of Behemoth (the hippopotamus or a mythological counterpart) and Leviathan (the crocodile or a mythological counterpart).[38]

Because we cannot exhaust the humorous possibilities of Job, we will content ourselves with examining what seem to be the most obvious. The reader may discover further examples of humor during their reflection upon Job.

Mr. and Mrs. Job

After his devastation, the only family member remaining for Job is his wife, who is understandably bitter. Many interpreters have found this situation humorous, albeit from a chauvinistic standpoint. Her nagging presence seems further evidence of his misfortune. She adds to his problems by placing before him the temptation to which Satan had wagered he would yield.

The author's ability to combine brevity with provocative speech and colorful images enables their interaction to retain its irony and poignancy even after many readings. The brevity of Mrs. Job's response has inspired curiosity in interpreters throughout history. The Septuagint, an ancient translation of the Old Testament into Greek, provided Mrs. Job with a few extra lines. The targum of Job (the Aramaic translation of Job supplemented by rabbinic comments) gives her the name Dinah. Perhaps the author's reason for keeping the dialogue brief was to encourage our participation in the text. What would we have said in his or her position? What was our response when in a similar situation? What does this reveal about us? How would God perceive the reactions of Job and his wife?

With Friends Like These...

Taken literally, Job's confrontation with his friends is hardly humorous. We would not consider the prospect of four adults at each other's throats to be food for laughter. Yet, when left to the imagination, we find a scenario that is quite conducive to humor.

What if the confrontation between Job and the friends were to be staged or filmed, with believable comical actors playing the friends? For the role of Job, the late Jackie Gleason, the "Poor Soul" himself, comes to mind. His ability to pop out his eyeballs, wiggle his nose, and make other descriptive facial gestures would have been quite comical. Art Carney would serve nicely as one of the friends, if only for his rapport with Gleason and his equally humorous body movements.[39] The other two roles are less obvious and would depend on one's preferences for actors. Regardless of our choices, the potential for a humorous and outrageous scene is considerable: four adults insulting, scolding, and threatening each other with loaded phrases, colorful analogies, and sophisticated God-talk. It is hard to imagine four people speaking this way only until you get into such a situation. Then the opportunity arises to laugh at your own behavior.

The Friends Eat Their Words

I would have enjoyed seeing the looks on the friends' faces when Yahweh tells them: "I'm angry with you, and you will need Job's intercession. Go to him and ask for his prayers." They must have been stunned! Could they have believed their ears? What tortuous, humiliating thoughts must have gone through their minds as they prepared to petition Job to intercede for them! We who have endured their pompous lecturing of Job laugh to ourselves as we visualize them receiving their comeuppance. We can imagine the type of reception they expected to get from Job: ridicule, "I-told-you-so's," a condescending chuckle. Imagine the surprise on their faces when Job refused to exploit their vulnerability by crowing over his vindication. What a model of evangelization he was for them! All this from an apparently condemned man.

Thanks, God, But No Thanks

While Job was going through the wringer of suffering, it became increasingly obvious that he needed some sort of break or relief. In ironic fashion, he receives human consolation only when his most urgent need has passed. The mischievous and skeptical part of ourselves can't help but wonder why Job didn't think, even for a second, the following thought: "Why me? Why now? Where were you when I really needed you? Why give me good comforters only when my main source of pain (your absence) is gone? What lousy timing!" While Job as an obedient servant of Yahweh apparently did not think twice, we, his imperfect descendants, might have raised a question or two.

From a humorous perspective there is a subtle problem with the ending: it's too smooth. It would have been comical and faithful to human nature for Job to stand up to God and respond to his twofold restoration[40] as follows: "God, thanks but no thanks! Too much has happened to me recently. I appreciate the offer, but I'd rather stay poor and isolated as I am. I prefer to keep my expectations low and avoid being so vulnerable. Were my fortunes to tumble once more, I couldn't bear going through the same disappointment."

After dealing with such a mysterious and transcendent God, who gives and takes away according to the incomprehensible divine plan, we could hardly blame Job if he asked for a breather. We could reason that he was too shell-shocked to accept the possibility of another such experience. Yet, the story ends with Job enjoying his new-found prosperity, including three beautiful daughters. What does Job know that we don't? What motivates him to live life so enthusiastically,[41] even when he is fully aware of how absurd and painful it can be?

Acceptance

Quite simply, Job has learned to live with God and life. He no longer draws lines, imposes rules, or dictates circumstances. He has decided to go with the flow, and enjoy life as much as possible. He respects God's freedom, and is glad that God respects his. Most important, Job has let go of the pride which not only got in the way of his relationship with God, but stifled his sense of humor as well. After all that had happened, he could no longer take himself, life, or religion too seriously. He was too busy looking at the world from God's joyful perspective to get wrapped up in trivialities. If God wanted to shower him with gifts, fine; if not, that's fine too. Job still might complain, but at least he'd know God was on his side, and that there was a mysterious design and plan behind the madness.

It is only fitting that the story concludes with Job celebrating with his family and friends, and eventually dying at a ripe old age. Once we have learned to accept both good and bad from the hand of divine providence and human freedom, confident of God's faithfulness and mercy, the time we would have spent fretting can now be used to smile and enjoy life to the best of our ability. For Job, life was too long to spend it quarreling with God, the best friend and comforter that he had.

Humor Begins at Home

It is easy to advise others to discover humor in their situation and to accept the hand of providence in both positive and negative circumstances. The real test is whether we struggle to apply these principles in our own lives. The book of Job is helpful for coping with suffering because it presents both positive and negative aspects of life in an objective and balanced manner. It integrates intensity with humor, and profundity with common sense. It was written to help believers affirm the truth of their emotions and experiences without losing faith or hope. It blazes a path for care-givers and sufferers to follow in coping with life's insecurities, contradictions, disappointments, and tragedies without losing appreciation of its joys and wonders. It accomplishes this without forcing its opinion or doctrines upon us. Instead, it invites us to consider how we look upon suffering, care-giving, prosperity, justice, and personal integrity in the light of our religious beliefs and personal life vision.

Job is a holistic model of human potential, vocation, and care-giving that is greatly relevant in these troubled and uncertain times. The challenge for sufferers and care-givers is to discover, actualize, and share its positive message in a culture that will resist it even though society's current value system and modus operandi have been proved inadequate and in dire need of transformation. In our final chapter, we will explore the possibility of introducing a Judeo-Christian spiritual growth and healing framework into personal, pastoral, and professional care-giving situations without discriminating against those who follow different values and belief systems.

Reflection Questions

Humor

How would you define humor?

How can you inject more humor into your personal life and personality? Consider both its amused and enthused aspects, as well as its application in relationships and interactions with others.

In the context of your personality and care-giving circumstances, how can you assume a more humorous disposition?

How can you use humor to heal others, peers, and yourself?

CHAPTER SEVEN

Therapeutic Applications of Job

Foundational Principles

In spiritual therapy it is crucial that we convey to sufferers, family members, and peers that we are not trying to impose our personal spirituality or philosophy on them, just as we wouldn't want theirs force-fitted on us. We are not using the story of Job to support our personal perspective or spirituality, but to help individuals (including ourselves) heal, reconcile, and grow. We don't employ Job, the Bible, or any inspired religious text to prove our point; rather, we try to understand how their practical wisdom, human values, compelling stories, and inspirational message might help the particular individual(s) to whom we minister. We always begin by listening, serving, and discerning.

We will make mistakes and misjudgments in spiritual therapy as we do in all areas of life: e.g. work, family, friendships, morality, health, etc. These mistakes may yield consequences for others as well. Incorporating spirituality into care-giving is an inexact learning process which will be challenging for all parties concerned. Internalizing and applying the values of Job and religion/spirituality is a gradual, sometimes painful therapy in a culture that craves instant, painless relief. However, the benefits of spirituality greatly outweigh the costs, and the alternative of pure secularism has been demonstrated to be far worse: witness the extraordinary levels of substance abuse, violence, economic exploitation, juvenile delinquency, and suicide which emanate from the materialistic values and personal meaning vacuum created by society's general rejection of Judeo-Christian values.

Explicit and Implicit Applications of Job

Throughout this work, we have interwoven explicit and implicit applications of Job without distinguishing the two. Generic or implicit concepts from Job (e.g. personal meaning, persistence, integrity, trust, listening, reconciliation, etc.) may be the care-giver's primary Joban resource when working in a secular environment. Opportunities to utilize passages or images from Job explicitly will be less common for a variety of reasons, the most prominent of which being time constraints and pastoral sensitivity. Many sufferers will not be interested in or ready for Job. In such cases, the care-giver can draw on the aforementioned implicit concepts as a means of ministering to the sufferer's spiritual needs.

The Role of *Lectio Divina* in the Healing Vocations

Individuals who are attracted to Job's message and images may find *lectio divina* to be the healing or catalyzing agent their spirit needs. In *Where Is God When You Need Him?* there is a detailed overview of *lectio divina,* the ancient monastic model for absorbing, internalizing, and entering into dialogue with the word of God. The objective of this chapter is to explain how *lectio divina* can be used to foster spirituality (first and foremost), healing, and personal growth.

Lectio divina is appropriate in health-care and pastoral care as a holistic method of personal and spiritual growth. It can help individuals slow down, center themselves in their core beliefs and values, and take stock of their current situation. It can also function as a type of spiritual and emotional catharsis, enabling persons to get to the roots of their feelings and express them in a constructive manner before God, the master care-giver.

Because *lectio divina* is ultimately a very basic and fluid process, it does not require extensive instruction, nor does it marry one to a mechanical technique. While traditionally the Bible and secondarily the writings of the fathers of the early church have been the texts used in *lectio divina*, its framework has also been applied to other spiritual literature. For care-giving purposes, its boundaries need not stop there. The framework of *lectio divina* is suitable for responding to all events, relationships, persons, and other stimuli (e.g. nature) in which we may have sensed God's presence, absence, or providence. It can be applied to all human experiences that offer the potential of contemplative reflection.

This versatility and universality is its main link to care-giving. Care-givers can encourage individuals who do not wish to use the Bible or other spiritual literature to enter into some event, element of nature, personal memory, relationship, or a particular poem, quote, or book that holds meaning for them, and engage in a dialogue with it. Any stimuli that can help the sufferer or care-giver work through painful circumstances and be transformed, even slightly, in the process is an excellent subject for *lectio divina*. The four steps of *lectio divina* (reading/listening, meditation, prayer, and contemplation) are so basic to human nature that they are applicable potentially to almost anything of consequence within the realm of human experience. Fr. Luke Dysinger's article in the appendix offers a practical model for applying *lectio divina* to life experiences.

The following examples will illustrate the diverse ways in which *lectio divina* can be applied in care-giving situations:

Lectio Divina in Practice

Coping with Questions

The role of questioning and communications as a path to contemplation has been dramatized by the book of Job. Because care-givers are often confronted with essentially unanswerable questions by sufferers (e.g.: Why did God take my wife at so young an age? Why did God permit my brother to be killed by a drunk driver?), Job is a most appropriate resource, for if there is anyone who poses unanswerable questions, it is Job. How might *lectio divina* be utilized in response to painful questions posed by sufferers?

While Job raises many thought-provoking questions, his first question stands out as perhaps the most fundamental and controversial for sufferers: "We accept good things from God; and should we not accept evil?"[42] We will consider this question in the context of the pastoral care scenario that follows.

The Innocent Sufferer

Marie is a thoughtful woman in her early forties who is going through a painful divorce initiated by her husband. Her husband is an ambitious businessman who has not put the effort into their marriage that he has put into his profession. Marie loves her husband deeply, and does not understand how their communication channels became so clogged. While she acknowledges her role in the breakdown of the relationship, she is heartbroken over her husband's unwillingness to try to heal the marriage.

Because her faith has always played a central role in her life, she brings her questions and anguish to God, yet receives no answers or consolations. In a case of innocent suffering such as Marie's, it is fruitless to provide rational explanations or consolations for her tragedy. The only therapy that works is touch, listening, and sharing in the pain.

Marie's religious formation was based on answers and order. Life went according to certain religious and moral formulas that were predicated on human cooperation. If you were faithful to God, you would be rewarded; if not, you would be punished either by God or by natural consequences. Paralleling her acceptance of the disciplinary initiative of God was a sincere faith in his omnipotence and providence. Well, she exclaims to her care-giver, how could God permit this to happen? Marie is currently experiencing spiritual unrest that is doing her physical and emotional harm.

An individual like Marie who has a reasonably mature faith and is emotionally stable may be receptive to the concept of redemptive suffering. Of course, in the case of unstable individuals or those overwrought with grief, mention of this would be imprudent and likely to incur ridicule and rage. The loaded question previously cited from Job could be shared with Marie to affirm that the ultimate test of human integrity and faithfulness is innocent suffering. As discussed in *Where Is God When You Need Him?* the central challenge of Job is that of unconditional love and fidelity. Will Marie continue to love God and herself, and eventually forgive her husband, even when she feels no rational or emotional justification? The care-giver could refer to God's testing of Job's disinterested service in the prologue and Job's faithful response despite having great incentive to follow the lead of his wife and curse God.[43] When Marie gets angry and wishes to voice her distress to God, the laments of Job may serve as permission and inspiration. Marie could be instructed that if it helps her cope with her pain, it is perfectly in accordance with the biblical tradition to conceive of herself as being tested for no humanly discernible reason,[44] and therefore presented with the opportunity of loving God "for nothing."[45]

If such an approach is taken, it is essential that Marie be reminded that unconditional love is an ideal that she has the rest of her life to work toward. It is perfectly acceptable if she needs time to work through her anger and sadness. What she needs to draw from this identification with Job is that God loves her dearly, and holds her in higher esteem than she can imagine. Somehow he will bring her through this. Faith testifies that God can bring good out of this sad event.[46]

Neither Marie, nor Job, nor anyone else can comprehend fully how suffering fits into God's eternal plan. All Marie can do is exercise unconditional love, however imperfect, toward God, herself, and her husband, which includes avoiding excessive introspection and hindsight. Accepting evil/bad things as part of God's permissive will and mysterious providence will require her whole self, body, mind, and spirit. To withstand the stress, Marie may need to get exercise and keep physically and socially active (if only to divert her attention from her trauma), as well as develop some inspiring personal mottos, sayings, or affirmations that she can repeat to herself daily. Perhaps she could use a quote from the Bible or some other literature which gives her strength. She needs to follow Job's example in sharing consistently and persistently her feelings with God, while keeping in mind God's affirmation of Job in 42:7-9, which she could justifiably apply to herself. Rather than seek answers to her painful ordeal, Marie can strive to live life's challenging questions, particularly the call to accept on faith both joy and sorrow as mysterious elements of divine providence.

Theological Undertones

As a footnote to our discussion of Job's thought-provoking statement, we can recall that Hebrew, unlike Latin and Greek, had no word for suffering. The Hebrew word in verse 2:10 commonly translated as evil or "bad things" in this context refers to the disasters and calamities of life rather than to moral evil.[47] Of course, human suffering is evil in the sense that it was not part of the original plan of the Creator. Theological language used to discuss the mystery of evil/suffering is rather complex, and we best refer to theological textbooks, church statements, or biblical commentaries for a more precise treatment. Care-givers who wish to experience the primitive origins of this language as expressed in narrative form can study and reflect upon the first eleven chapters of Genesis, particularly chapters 1 through 4. When read in the manner of Job as an existential story with practical applications for daily life, the book of Genesis communicates timeless truths about human existence that provide an excellent context for going deeper into the questions raised by Job. Like Job, the early chapters of Genesis narrate the fundamental questions and dilemmas which have challenged believers from all creeds and cultures throughout history. It is not surprising that chapter 3 of Job borrows the language of chapter 1 of Genesis to describe Job's existential anguish, and that other parts of Job reflect the influence of Genesis as well.

The Angry Sufferer

Jeff is an angry man in his late twenties who has just received a diagnosis of cancer. The doctors cannot give him a good estimate of the chances of it going into remission. Jeff has had a relatively difficult life, but now is starting to settle down into a life pattern with which he is comfortable. He likes his job, makes a good salary, and recently has set a wedding date for a year from now. Jeff is a practicing Catholic who was raised, like Job, to believe that God rewards those who obey the divine commandments. Jeff is experiencing severe guilt over areas of sinfulness in his life (it is only Job who can claim a skeleton-free closet) because he believes that these may be partially responsible for his affliction. Jeff uses harsh language in speaking about God, and is unreceptive to all efforts to explain his suffering through either traditional theology (God's direct and permissive will) or modern naturalistic philosophy (suffering is a natural part of human existence that occurs independent of God's will). He takes the initiative with care-givers in talking about God, but does very little listening.

With an explosive individual like Jeff, the last thing a care-giver should consider is a frontal assault. Do not confront Jeff on his theological turf; his defenses are entrenched too deeply. However, we can circumvent these defenses by being patient with Jeff and demonstrating our support through empathetic listening. The only way Jeff will open himself spiritually to another is by that individual gaining his trust. When Jeff is convinced that his anger and outrage are respected, he will be more willing to listen.

Because Jeff is an energetic and intense individual who has always lived life to the full, he can relate to certain dynamic aspects of creation such as nature. Because of his painful past, he is aware of the fragility of life and the perplexing futility of human efforts. He might be able to enter into the spirituality of the Yahweh speeches (chapters 38-41), which draw the listener into a deeper appreciation of the wonders of creation. By devoting some time to quiet reflection, Jeff may discover that there is some order and purpose to life, however chaotic it may seem, but this order must ultimately be accepted on faith.

To internalize this awareness, Jeff could practice *lectio divina* on selections from the Yahweh speeches which describe awe-inspiring aspects of nature. By reading, repeating, affirming, visualizing, praying, and contemplating these verses, and responding to his insights in a practical way (e.g. by committing himself to spend some time each week alone in nature), Jeff might gain perspective on his affliction, and learn to trust that although there is a significant element of chaos in his life, God is still mysteriously in charge. Although Jeff, like Job, will still have his doubts, he can channel his intensity in a creative way and begin the process of reconciliation by starting with nature, perhaps the least threatening of the basic human relationships (as mentioned previously, the others being with God, self, and other persons).

As a follow-up to his reflections, Jeff could read chapter 28 of Job, and perhaps enter into it through *lectio divina* with the following twist: Rewrite the wisdom poem using his own experience. How have God and life surpassed his expectations in the past and revealed to him how futile are his attempts at truly comprehending the more profound events of life? Have there been times when he has agonized over realities that have never come to pass, or which turned out much better than he expected? Has he had any prior experience of God's surpassing wisdom and providence that gives him hope that God will not abandon him? Jeff may rest easier when he realizes that much of life is beyond his control and understanding, and the best he can do is follow the counsel of verse 28:28 of Job: fear/revere the Lord and avoid evil.

Jeff needs guidance and support in leaving his familiar turf. Empowered by care-giver patience, gentleness, and respect, Jeff can choose to open himself to other persons and God. His natural attributes of intensity and enthusiasm will aid him in carrying out this decision.

The Depressed Sufferer

Frank is an individual with no religious affiliation who is despondent over a personal loss. He is dwelling on the loss in an obsessive manner that is beginning to affect his health. He appears listless and apathetic. Anything which can divert his attention from his loss will be helpful.

In such a case, the care-giver might try to learn from Frank what aspects of life speak most to his heart, and suggest that he spend some time becoming immersed in those realities. This is not offered as an escape, but as a centering tool which may help Frank regain perspective and activate his core beliefs and values. What motivates Frank, and helps him to get through difficult times?

A basic explanation of the stages of *lectio divina* substituting equivalent secular terminology for the religious language can provide Frank with the basics for getting started. For example, the terms absorbing, internalizing, and dialoguing can be used.

In using the term dialoguing in place of prayer and contemplation, the emphasis will be on Frank expressing his thoughts and feelings about the stimuli, and then listening in silence for the reaction stirred within his heart. The religious roots of this adaptation of *lectio divina* can be explained briefly and with sensitivity. Frank must understand that his religious views are respected, and that the framework of *lectio divina* is suggested solely for his personal benefit.

The Searching Sufferer

Cindy is an evangelical Protestant who has lost a child and is furious with God, though she downplays her anger. Her relationship with her husband has been strained by this loss, and there is an underlying air of tension between them. Friends from her church have been very sensitive and supportive, with the exception of one of her closer friends who has engaged in simplistic God-talk at inopportune times. Her unsophisticated and casual use of the terms "God's will," "Offer it up," and "The Lord's doing what's best" has hurt and confused Cindy, who is not sure what to believe.

Cindy has consulted her pastor about her confusion, and he has taken the common modern approach that God is her friend and healer, but he had nothing to do with the loss endured by Cindy. When Cindy asks the typical questions concerning God's omnipotence and providence, the pastor states that God has given human beings freedom to do both good and evil, and has placed natural laws into effect that govern the cycles of nature. God can't be held responsible for death resulting from natural or human causes. Her pastor explains that death is a mysterious reality of life which she must accept rather than struggle with or question. Further reflection will only depress and frustrate her.

Cindy is glad that her pastor did not bludgeon her with a lecture on original sin or remind her that the wages of sin is death. She was also glad not to hear that heaven is a gift to those who were faithful to God on earth. In her situation such theological concepts are little consolation. Cindy is not looking for answers, but for a way to live with herself, her husband, and God in view of the tragic loss of her child. On the rational level, she understands that death claims persons of all ages, but emotionally she asks, "Why me? What did I do? What did my child do to deserve this? Is there no order or justice?" Cindy is depressed, and has spent considerably less time in church and in private prayer. Fortunately, she relieves some of her stress through physical exercise.

In the context of a support group or direct one-to-one counseling, Cindy might benefit from the first three chapters of Job. Most important for Cindy, assuming that her counselor or minister feels she is emotionally and spiritually ready for such an intense experience, is to enter into the pain of Job and his wife. When she sees that even a perfect person like Job squabbles with his spouse in response to the tragic loss of children, she will understand that the pressures on her and her husband are almost unbearable, and that it is understandable that their relationship has suffered. She might also benefit from reflecting on the pain of Mrs. Job, and perhaps identifying with it. She may need to follow Mrs. Job in speaking harshly about God and the demands of faith, if that is how she feels. Hopefully she will come to realize that in entering into the words and emotions of

Mrs. Job, she is also encountering God's word, and that by being honest about her anger, and sharing with God the depth of her feelings, she is honoring him, and treating him as a friend. She can take comfort from God's affirmation of Job's truthfulness,[48] and consider it permission to follow in his blunt footsteps.

The speeches of Job's friends would be helpful to the extent that she can perceive the similarity in attitude between Job's friends and her friend. She could discover this resemblance by reading just one or two speeches of the friends, and thereby avoid the boring repetition and intense theological subtlety which marks their discourses. She needs to recognize that even devoutly religious people are susceptible to callousness and insensitivity, and that though they might claim to speak for God, their authority is self-imposed. It would be helpful for her to note both God's correction of the God-talking friends and his expectation that Job will offer intercession for them. She could derive from this that God wills that she ignore the misguided God-talk, and eventually understand and forgive her friend.

Different Quotes for Different Folks

Because each individual is different, no one way of practicing *lectio divina* is appropriate for all. Further, each person will have a different reaction to individual biblical texts and teachings based on past experiences, personality, current mood, and personal beliefs. People also have different tolerances of intensity. In our previous example, Cindy may be able to identify with Job's misfortune and join him in mourning over the loss of their children. She may even be able to share her pain with her husband, and together they could pray either Job's defiant or obedient words, depending on how the Spirit moves them. Another individual in Cindy's position may be able to relate to Job only after years of the healing and reconciliation process.

Vocational Therapy for Care-Givers

Keeping in mind the mounting pressures and expectations facing the care-giver, we will now consider how Job and *lectio divina* can speak to the care-giver's vocational situation. Two citations from Job with parallel themes come immediately to mind (though there are many more that could be chosen). First, verse 3:20: "Why is light given to the toilers, and life to the bitter in spirit?"; second, verses 7:11-12: "Is not man's life on earth a drudgery? Are not his days those of a hireling? He is a slave who longs for the shade, a hireling who waits for his wages."

In light of the simple but profound message of these verses, it might be helpful to pause over these briefly, and reflect upon the timeless truth they contain. These verses hold particular relevance for care-givers who suffer while fulfilling their vocation. At times, the care-giving vocation is neither healthy nor fulfilling. Rising responsibilities, time constraints, and insufficient resources can color the care-giver's entire experience of life. Work can seem like fruitless toil, thus bringing to mind the curse imposed on human work in Genesis 3:17-19.

When we encounter these and other sober verses in *lectio divina,* we empower ourselves to deal more responsibly with the difficult truths and realities of life. Not only care-givers, but all human beings have known the experience of hard work yielding a disproportionately small harvest. This is a mystery that can tear one apart if confronted solely at the rational level. Fortunately, we can release intense and volatile emotions by bringing them to prayer and contemplation, and thereby open ourselves to God's healing power and wisdom. There may be many difficult days when we can recall these timeless words of Job, and temporarily retreat into reflection and prayer to gain sustenance and hope.

Bringing these verses to *lectio divina* along with our feelings and experience will not necessarily solve or improve our situation; rather, it will provide us with the strength to discover and affirm the truth about our circumstances, and resolve to persevere in our integrity to the best of our ability. Such honesty is a far superior alternative to incessant griping, rage, or repression of our painful emotions and experiences. In *lectio divina,* we bring our vocational pain before the divine healer who can heal not only through scripture and other spiritual texts, but through nature, persons, events, and personal memories as well.

Lectio Divina in Small But Powerful Doses

It is worth reinforcing that when sharing the possibility of *lectio divina,* we must keep our care-giving instructions simple and basic. Many people have difficulty with complex methods or theology, and are more comfortable with simple explanations and tasks. In these cases, a single verse or two from Job, the psalms (a particularly good source), or other biblical or inspirational literature may inspire enough meaning and insight to occupy the individual in time of reflection. Rhythmic repetition of a verse or phrase can help us internalize its message, and foster its penetration into the subconscious mind. Certain verses may be so relevant to our personal situation and history that we choose to linger over that verse, and enter into its depth of meaning in a gradual manner. We may find it helpful to periodically return to these verses for inspiration and consolation.

The Place of *Lectio Divina* in Health-Care and Pastoral Care

From a practical perspective, *lectio divina* is appropriate in health-care because it fosters self-understanding, honest expression of emotions, holistic participation in the healing process, and reconciliation. Because of its generic theological and anthropological concepts, the framework of *lectio divina* can be adapted by persons of non-Judeo-Christian belief systems. When dealing with such persons, the care-giver must be open to possible applications to their situation. Humble and prudent attempts to help individuals relate to God, whether through inspired texts, sacraments or rituals, nature, other persons, music, memories, etc., are appropriate in both secular and pastoral contexts. Like Job, some individuals will be satisfied only by an encounter with God. *Lectio divina* is there as a support for people who want to put their questions, confusion, hurt, and anger before God, however they conceive of him. It is a superior alternative to giving people easy answers or ignoring their spiritual unrest.

In our enthusiasm for its healing and transformational possibilities, we must keep in mind that *lectio divina* is not a wonder therapy that is appropriate in all circumstances; our point is that it may be helpful in some care-giving situations. We must temper any zealousness for its application with the following question: If I were in their position, would I want to reflect on God's word, or would I prefer simply to be shown compassion and understanding?

Sensitive utilization of *lectio divina* does not impinge on personal space, nor does it artificially introduce spirituality into an unrelated realm. Only with insensitive, prideful, or aggressive application does it pose a threat either to individual rights or to the healing process. Its main prerequisite is a sufficient level of spiritual and psychological maturity on the part of both sufferer and care-giver. Individuals are at various stages of readiness to encounter God, reality, or themselves during situations of suffering. In such cases, we can recall the example of the master care-giver, God, and follow in his patient, humorous, sensitive, and compassionate footsteps.

Not for Experts Only

It is unrealistic and inefficient to assign all spiritual care-giving to clergy, chaplains, and pastoral care-givers. Of course, to avoid the opposite extreme of reckless and misguided application, *lectio divina* must be understood and practiced in some form by the care-giver. Before we even consider sharing *lectio divina* with another person, we must be convinced of its efficacy and therapeutic potential.

While we must be aware of our spiritual care limitations,

and refer complex situations to trained personnel, we also need to reach out in simple ways when we discern the Spirit calling us forth. Because such matters of discernment can be quite complicated, we need to conduct an ongoing dialogue with other individuals trying to facilitate spiritual healing. This helps us maintain a degree of objectivity and mutual support. With study, prayer, reflection, mutual support, and experience, the caregiver can develop the discernment, compassion, and tact necessary for helping disposed individuals of all belief systems to experience spiritual healing and personal growth.

When faced with mistakes due to misguided judgments and inexperience, it is essential to recall that it is not results, important as they are, that ultimately must motivate the caregiver, but sincere intent and compassionate actions. We are instruments rather than the cure. We are only responsible to do our best. As a sufferer, I would much prefer a care-giver who takes care of my practical needs, and is concerned (though not overbearing!) about my spiritual needs, than a care-giver who wishes to do the bare minimum, and avoids anything that would entail risk and intense involvement in my pain.

Authors and practitioners such as Bernie Siegel, Norman Cousins, Viktor Frankl, Joan Borysenko, Carl O. Simonton, and Herbert Benson have demonstrated that the human spirit is a powerful factor in the healing process. If we accept secular personal health and growth concepts as part of holistic therapy, why disregard spiritual or religious ones in situations where the patient or family desires them? Subordinating, manipulating, or summarily rejecting spiritual therapy due to religious prejudice of any kind discriminates against the patient and obstructs the healing process.

Motives for Introducing *Lectio Divina*

Both Job and *lectio divina* are valuable therapeutic instruments appropriate for sharing with all persons who demonstrate interest and need. Job can be therapeutic if it serves only to facilitate deeper communication between sufferer and care-giver. Many individuals will perceive Job as inspiring rather than as inspired literature. Whether one views it as the word of God, the word of humanity, or the mysterious interaction of both, no one can credibly discount its potential for good when used in a nonjudgmental and prudent manner.

When we use either *lectio divina* or Job in a care-giving context, the relevant criteria and questions are: Is our primary motive a care-giving rather than a sectarian religious one? Are we trying to build up the individual by providing therapy for the whole person according to *their* needs and objectives, rather than ours? We must endeavor to keep our ego, biases, and personal agendas at bay, and in the process meet the physical, emotional, and spiritual needs of the sufferer.

Sufferers are drawn to Job for a variety of reasons. I might have experienced a succession of misfortunes and subsequent lack of support from friends that causes me to identify with Job as he sits on the dung heap. Perhaps I am angry with God, my worshiping community, or religious institution, and consciously or subconsciously desire to express my emotions and experiences. I might be a grieving person who needs permission to ventilate difficult emotions. Perhaps I am trying to discover meaning in my circumstances, and the Joban concept of redemptive or intercessory suffering[49] gives me something to live for.

Those with a negative self-image may benefit from the positive anthropology found in the book of Job: Job stands up to God and receives divine praise for his honesty. In fact, an often overlooked constructive use of the Bible in care-giving involves individual self-esteem. The Bible attributes a challenging potential and call to each person that we would not dare to express were it not inscribed in God's word. For example, Genesis 1:26-27 speaks of humanity as being made in God's image and likeness, while Psalm 8 states that we are little lower than the angels.[50] We can observe the pride God shows in Job in the prologue, and assume God feels the same way about us. Through the process of *lectio divina,* we can affirm and visualize the dignity and uniqueness of each person (including ourselves!), and the delight and pride that God has in all individuals. We do not need to convey our vision to the sufferer by words (though at times explicit sharing is appropriate) or (God forbid) preaching; our actions and manner will speak volumes.

Reflection Questions

Job as Therapy

Do you feel lectio divina *in either standard or modified form might be helpful in certain care-giving situations? Why or why not?*

Consider how in a typical care-giving situation you might utilize lectio divina *or some aspect or modification of it.*

Do you feel called or drawn to practice lectio divina *in your personal life? If so, how will you respond to this call?*

Conclusion

Job as Therapy

Among all the books of the Bible, Job is most appropriate for use in a secular therapeutic setting. Its society of admirers includes famous and anonymous individuals from all walks of life, both secular and religious. Sufferers need to tell their story, and hear the stories of others. They need to teach and heal others even as they learn and are healed. Job provides a context in which sufferers can conceive and visualize their story played out against a mysterious and providential background. When used in an ecumenical manner, Job's positive message can provide inspiration, hope, and spiritual companionship for disposed sufferers.

Job and spirituality may not be politically expedient in some situations, but they contain a tremendous potential for healing. Job offers hope and motivation in a dramatically personal as well as universal way. This personal aspect is a distinguishing characteristic of Job and the Bible that is especially efficacious when we are suffering or care-giving. I am Job, we are Job. In Job, disposed individuals can discover a word or message to motivate, comfort, and encourage them in their situation. Such personal meaning can rejuvenate and inspire both sufferers and care-givers as they struggle to cope with mysteries that defy rational explanation and call for the best in both individuals and communities.

Notes

1. Viktor E. Frankl, *Man's Search for Meaning* (New York: Washington Square Press, 1984) 141-142.
2. In the sense of timelessness and universality, speaking the questions and concerns of individuals from all eras, cultures and perspectives.
3. Cf. Jb 25:4-6.
4. In light of society's predominant rejection of the interior life (prayer and contemplation) in favor of a seemingly more productive activism, it is not surprising that "burn-out" is so prevalent today.
5. That is, a revelatory presence of God.
6. Cf. Jb 42:7-9.
7. In the literal sense of the Latin root **educo**, to lead out.
8. Cf. Jb 40:6–41:26.
9. Cf. Jb 40:15.
10. Cf. Jb 2:13.
11. Cf. Jb 42:7-9.
12. Cf. Jb 9:33; 16:9; 19:25. This arbiter is possibly God himself, though scholarly opinion varies. The text is not specific enough to draw any firm conclusions.
13. Retribution doctrine held that God eventually rewards the just and punishes the wicked. Since, at the time Job was written, there was no defined Jewish belief in an afterlife other than in the hazy domain of Sheol, these rewards and punishments were expected in this life, rather than in the hereafter.
14. In certain situations, the care-giver may discern that the suf-

ferer needs to be challenged. Moral correction in times of suffering must be carried out with sensitivity to the psychological state of the sufferer. Assurance of God's forgiveness and mercy as well as one's personal support must accompany any correction, so that the hopefully repentant party can retain confidence and hope.

15. For a treatment of the states of orientation, disorientation, and new orientation in the context of the psalms, literature with much in common with Job, cf. Walter Brueggemann's *The Message of the Psalms,* published by Augsburg Publishing House.

16. Cf. Jb 19:28-29.

17. Cf. Jb 24:12.

18. Whether Job was actually aware of the wisdom poem is a matter of scholarly debate. The text is unclear as to the source of the poem. It could be an editorial observation by the narrator or a speech on the lips of Job or one of his friends. The vagueness and corruption of the Hebrew text renders all answers inconclusive. Our inference of Job's dissatisfaction with the poem derives from our viewing the book as a continuous whole in the form in which it has come down to us. We propose that the author placed it between the dialogue and Job's final testimony to mark it as a partial but incomplete explanation of the problem of innocent suffering.

19. Cf. Jb 30:10: "They abhor me, they stand aloof from me, they do not hesitate to spit in my face!"

20. Cf. Jb 32:1.

21. Old Testament imagery used to describe a theophany or mysterious and revelatory presence of God.

22. This work's classification of Elihu as a charismatic prophet reflects the insight of Walter Vogels as contained in his *Reading & Preaching the Bible: A New Semiotic Approach,* published by Michael Glazier. The reader of this chapter may wish to consult pages 80-103 of that work for an alternative treatment of the language used in Job for speaking about suffering.

23. Note that in St. Matthew's last judgement scene neither the righteous nor the wicked recognized God's presence in the suffering persons they were assisting or ignoring (cf. Mt 25:31-46.)

24. Cf. Jb 42:1-6 where Job contrasts hearsay or second-hand faith with the personal experience of God obtained through contemplation and the grace of divine revelation.

25. *Lectio divina* is the Latin term for the holistic approach to praying and applying God's word practiced by contemplative Christians since the fourth century.

26. Cf. Jb 38-41.

27. Cf. Jb 42:1-6.

28. Cf. 1 Cor 13:1-3.

29. Cf. Jb 42:1-6.

30. Cf. Lk 23:34.

31. That is, not humor in the sense of ridicule or sarcasm, but humor designed to get them off their soapbox and appeal to their more compassionate and humble side.

32. Cf. Jb 1:8; 2:3; 42:7-9.

33. Cf. Jb 13:14-16.

34. Cf. Jb 7:20-21.

35. Cf. Jb 38–41.

36. Cf. Jb 31:35-37.

37. Cf. Jb 42:1-6.

38. See chapters 38–41 of Job.

39. Selecting actors is naturally subjective; those readers whose tastes differ, please substitute your preferences.

40. Cf. Jb 42:10.

41. Both the prologue and epilogue reveal that Job's family celebrates God's blessings in a party atmosphere.

42. Cf. Jb 2:10.

43. Cf. Jb 2:3.

44. Cf. Jb 2:3.

45. Cf. Jb 1:9.

46. Cf. Rom 8:28.

47. Cf. Norman C. Habel, *The Book of Job* (Philadelphia: Westminster Press, 1985) 96.

48. Cf. Jb 42:7-9.
49. Cf. Jb 42:7-9.
50. The Hebrew word **elohim** translated as angels in Ps 8:6 can also be rendered as God.

Appendix 1

Suggestions for Further Reading

Chapter One
Wherever We Go, We Bring Ourselves

Edward Le Joly, *Mother Teresa of Calcutta: A Biography*. New York: Harper & Row, 1983.

Mother Teresa, *Words to Love By...*Notre Dame: Ave Maria Press, 1983.

Kathryn Spink, *I Need Souls Like You: Sharing in the Work of Mother Teresa Through Prayer and Suffering*. New York: Harper & Row, 1984.

Chapter Two
The Therapeutic Power of Personal Meaning and the Human Spirit

Viktor E. Frankl, *The Will to Meaning: Foundations and Applications of Logotherapy*. New York: Meridian, 1988.

____, *Psychotherapy and Existentialism: Selected Papers on Logotherapy*. New York: Washington Square Press, 1985.

____, *Man's Search for Meaning*. New York: Washington Square Press, 1984.

_____, *The Unheard Cry for Meaning: Psychotherapy and Humanism.* New York: Washington Square Press, 1978.

Elisabeth Lukas, *Meaning in Suffering: Comfort in Crisis Through Logotherapy.* Berkeley: Institute of Logotherapy Press, 1985.

Donald F. Tweedie, *Logotherapy and the Christian Faith: An Evaluation of Frankl's Existential Approach to Psychotherapy.* Grand Rapids: Baker Book House, 1961.

Chapter Three
Models of Care-Giving

Gregory the Great, *Pastoral Care.* Ancient Christian Writers, no. 11, trans. Henry Davis. Mahwah: Paulist Press, 1950.

Pat McCloskey, *When You Are Angry With God.* Mahwah: Paulist Press, 1987.

Thomas C. Oden, *Care of Souls in the Classic Tradition.* Philadelphia: Fortress Press, 1984.

Pierre Wolff, I*s God Deaf?* Waldwick: Arena Lettres, 1984.

_____, *May I Hate God?* Mahwah: Paulist Press, 1979.

Chapter Four
The Language of Suffering and Care-Giving

Walter Brueggemann, *The Message of the Psalms.* Minneapolis: Augsburg Publishing House, 1984.

Anthony de Mello, *Sadhana: A Way to God.* New York: Image Books, 1984.

Thomas Keating, *Open Mind, Open Heart.* New York: Amity House, 1986.

_____, M. Basil Pennington, and Thomas E. Clark, *Finding Grace at the Center.* Petersham: St. Bede's Publications, 1978.

Carlo M. Martini, *Praying with Saint Luke.* Dublin: Veritas, 1987.

M. Basil Pennington, *Centered Living: The Way of Centering Prayer.* Garden City: Doubleday & Company, Inc., 1986.

Walter E. Vogels, *Reading & Preaching the Bible: A New Semiotic Approach.* Wilmington: Michael Glazier, 1986.

Chapter Five
Trust and Integrity: Essential Care-Giver Dispositions

Vincent Dwyer, O.C.S.O., *Lift Your Sails: The Challenge of Being a Christian.* New York: Doubleday, 1987.

Jean Vanier, *Be Not Afraid.* Mahwah: Paulist Press, 1975.

Chapter Six
The Healing Possibilities of Humor

Henri Cormier, *The Humor of Jesus.* Staten Island: Alba House, 1977.

Joseph A. Grassi, *God Makes Me Laugh: A New Approach to Luke.* Wilmington: Michael Glazier, Inc., 1987.

Chapter Seven
Therapeutic Applications of Job

Thelma Hall, *Too Deep for Words: Rediscovering Lectio Divina.* Mahwah: Paulist Press, 1988.

Dom Jean Leclercq, *The Love of Learning and the Desire for God.* New York: Mentor Omega Books, 1962.

Wulstan Mork, *The Benedictine Way.* Petersham: St. Bede's Publications, 1987.

David E. Rosage, *What Scripture Says About Healing: A Guide to Scriptural Prayer and Meditation.* Ann Arbor: Servant Books, 1988.

Karl Schultz, *Where Is God When You Need Him?: Sharing Stories of Suffering With Job and Jesus.* Staten Island: Alba House, 1992.

"Job Therapy" Workshops

Karl Schultz offers workshops and retreats on care-giving and therapeutic applications of Job. The workshop *Job Therapy: The Art and Vocation of Care-Giving* was approved for 7.5 contact hours by the Pennsylvania Nurses Association, a constituent of the American Nurses Association. For information on *Job Therapy* and other personal/professional development workshops, contact Genesis Personal Development Center at (412) 486-6087, or write P.O. Box 201, Glenshaw, Pa 1511.

Appendix 2

Accepting the Embrace of God: The Ancient Art of Lectio Divina by Fr. Luke Dysinger, O.S.B.

The Process of *Lectio Divina*

A very ancient art, practiced at one time by all Christians, is the technique known as *lectio divina*—a slow, contemplative praying of the scriptures which enables the Bible, the word of God, to become a means of union with God. This ancient practice has been kept alive in the Christian monastic tradition, and is one of the precious treasures of Benedictine monastics and oblates. Together with the liturgy and daily manual labor, time set aside in a special way for *lectio divina* enables us to discover in our daily life an underlying spiritual rhythm. Within this rhythm we discover an increasing ability to offer more of ourselves and our relationships to the Father, and to accept the embrace that God is continuously extending to us in the person of his Son Jesus Christ.

Lectio—Reading/Listening

The art of *lectio divina* begins with cultivating the ability to listen deeply, to hear "with the ear of our hearts," as St. Benedict encourages us in the Prologue to the Rule. When we read the scriptures, we should try to imitate the prophets Elijah. We should allow ourselves to become women and men who are able to listen for the still, small voice of God (1 Kgs 19:12); the "faint murmuring sound" which is God's word for us, God's voice touching our hearts. This gentle listening is an "atunement" to the presence of God in that special part of God's creation which is the scriptures.

The cry of the prophets to ancient Israel was the joy-filled command to "Listen!" "Sh'ma Israel: Hear, O Israel!" In *lectio divina* we, too, heed that command and turn to the scriptures, knowing that, we must "hear"—listen—to the voice of God, which often speaks very softly. In order to hear someone speaking softly, we must learn to be silent. We must learn to love silence. If we are constantly speaking or if we are surrounded with noise, we cannot hear gentle sounds. The practice of *lectio divina*, therefore, requires that we first quiet down in order to hear God's word to us. This is the first step of *lectio divina*, appropriately called *lectio*—reading.

The reading or listening which is the first step in *lectio divina* is very different from the speed reading which modern Christians apply to newspapers, books and even to the Bible. *Lectio* is reverential listening; listening in a spirit both of silence and of awe. We are listening for the still, small voice of God that will speak to us personally—not loudly, but intimately. In *lectio* we read slowly, attentively, gently listening to hear a word or phrase that is God's word for us this day.

Meditatio—Meditation

Once we have found a word or passage in the scriptures which speaks to us in a personal way, we must take it in and "ruminate" on it. The image of the ruminant animal quietly chewing its cud was used in antiquity as a symbol of the Christian pondering the word of God. Christians have always seen an icon of *lectio divina* in the Blessed Virgin Mary "pondering in her heart" what she saw and heard of Christ (Lk 2:19). For us today these images are a reminder that we must take in the word—that is, memorize it—and while gently repeating it to ourselves, allow it to interact with our thoughts, our hopes, our memories, our desires. This is the second step or stage in *lectio divina–meditatio.* Through *meditatio* we allow God's word to become his word for us, a word that touches us and affects us at our deepest levels.

Oratio—Prayer

The third step in *lectio divina* is *oratio*—prayer: prayer understood both as dialogue with God, that is, as loving conversation with the one who has invited us into his embrace; and as consecration, prayer as the priestly offering to God of parts of ourselves that we have not previously believed God wants. In this consecration-prayer we allow the word that we have taken in and on which we are pondering to touch and change our deepest selves. Just as a priest consecrates the elements of bread and wine at the eucharist, God invites us in *lectio divina* to hold up our most difficult and pain-filled experiences to him, and to gently recite over them the healing word or phrase he has given us in our *lectio* and *meditatio*. In this *oratio*, this consecration-prayer, we allow our real selves to be touched and changed by the word of God.

Contemplatio—Contemplation

Finally, we simply rest in the presence of the one who has used his word as a means of inviting us to accept his transforming embrace. No one who has ever been in love needs to be reminded that there are moments in loving relationships when words are unnecessary. It is the same in our relationship with God. Wordless, quiet rest in the presence of the one who loves us has a name in the Christian tradition—*contemplatio*, contemplation. Once again we practice silence, letting go of our own words—this time simply enjoying the experience of being in the presence of God.

The Underlying Rhythm of *Lectio Divina*

If we are to practice *lectio divina* effectively, we must travel back in time to an understanding that today is in danger of being almost completely lost. In the Christian past the words *action* (or *practice,* from the Greek *praktikos*) and *contemplation* did not describe different kinds of Christians engaging (or not engaging) in different forms of prayer and apostolates. Practice and contemplation were understood as the two poles of our underlying, ongoing spiritual rhythm: a gentle oscillation back and forth between spiritual "activity" with regard to God and "receptivity."

Practice—spiritual activity—referred in ancient times to our active cooperation with God's grace in rooting out vices and allowing the virtues to flourish. The direction of spiritual activity was not outward in the sense of an apostolate, but inward—down into the depths of the soul where the Spirit of God is constantly transforming us, refashioning us in God's image. The active life is thus coming to see who we truly are and allowing ourselves to be remade into what God intends us to become.

In contemplation we cease from interior spiritual doing and learn simply to be, that is, to rest in the presence of our loving Father. Just as we constantly move back and forth in our exterior lives between speaking and listening, between questioning and reflecting, so in our spiritual lives we must learn to enjoy the refreshment of simply *being* in God's presence, an experience that naturally alternates (if we let it!) with our spiritual *practice.*

In ancient times contemplation was not regarded as a goal to be achieved through some method of prayer, but was simply accepted with gratitude as God's recurring gift. At intervals the Lord invites us to cease from speaking so that we can simply rest in his embrace. This is the pole of our inner spritual rhythm called contemplation.

How different this ancient understanding is from our modern approach! Instead of recognizing that we all gently oscillate back and forth between spiritual activity and receptivity, between practice and contemplation, we today tend to set contemplation before ourselves as a goal—something we imagine we can achieve through some spiritual technique. We must be willing to sacrifice our "goal-oriented" approach if we are to practice *lectio divina,* because *lectio divina* has no other goal than spending time with God through the medium of his word. The amount of time we spend in any aspect of *lectio divina*, whether it be rumination, consecration or contemplation, depends on God's Spirit, not on us. *Lectio divina* teaches us to savor and delight in all the different flavors of God's presence, whether they be active or receptive modes of experiencing him.

In *lectio divina* we offer ourselves to God; and we are people in motion. In ancient times this inner spiritual motion was described as a helix—an ascending spiral. Viewed in only two dimensions it appears as a circular motion back and forth; seen with the added dimension of time it becomes a helix, an ascending spiral by means of which we are drawn ever closer to God. The whole of our spiritual lives was viewed in this way, as a gentle oscillation between spiritual activity and receptivity by means of which God unites us ever closer to himself. In just the same way the steps or stages of *lectio divina* represent an oscillation back and forth between these spiritual poles. In *lectio divina* we recognize our underlying spiritual rhythm and discover many different ways of experiencing God's presence—many different ways of praying.

The Practice of *Lectio Divina*

Private *Lectio Divina*

Choose a text of the scriptures that you wish to pray. Many Christians use in their daily *lectio divina* one of the readings from the eucharistic liturgy for the day; others prefer to slowly work through a particular book of the Bible. It makes no difference which text is chosen, as long as one has no set goal of "covering" a certain amount of text: the amount of text "covered" is in God's hands, not yours.

Place yourself in a comfortable position and allow yourself to become silent. Some Christians focus for a few moments on their breathing; others have a beloved "prayer word" or "prayer phrase" they gently recite in order to become interiorly silent. For some the practice known as "centering prayer" makes a good, brief introduction to *lectio divina*. Use whatever method is best for you and allow yourself to enjoy silence for a few moments.

Then turn to the text and read it slowly, gently. Savor each portion of the reading, constantly listening for the "still, small voice" of a word or phrase that somehow says, "I am for you today." Do not expect lightning or ecstasies. In *lectio divina* God is teaching us to listen to him, to seek him in silence. He does not reach out and grab us; rather, he softly, gently invites us ever more deeply into his presence.

Next take the word or phrase into yourself. Memorize it and slowly repeat it to yourself, allowing it to interact with your inner world of concerns, memories and ideas. Do not be afraid of "distractions." Memories or thoughts are simply parts of yourself which, when they rise up during *lectio divina*, are asking to be given to God along with the rest of your inner self. Allow this inner pondering, this rumination, to invite you into dialogue with God.

Then, speak to God. Whether you use words or ideas or images or all three is not important. Interact with God as you would with one you know loves and accepts you. And give to him what you have discovered in yourself during your experience of *meditatio*. Experience yourself as the priest that you are. Experience God using the word or phrase that he has given you as a means of blessing, of transforming the ideas and memories, which your pondering on his word has awakened. Give to God what you have found within your heart.

Finally, simply rest in God's embrace. And when he invites you to return to your pondering of his word or to your inner dialogue with him, do so. Learn to use words when words are helpful, and to let go of words when they no longer are necessary. Rejoice in the knowledge that God is with you in both words and silence, in spiritual activity and inner receptivity.

Sometimes in *lectio divina* one will return several times to the printed text, either to savor the literary context of the word or phrase that God has given, or to seek a new word or phrase to ponder. At other times only a single word or phrase will fill the whole time set aside for *lectio divina*. It is not necessary to anxiously assess the quality of one's *lectio divina* as if one were "performing" or seeking some goal: *lectio divina* has no goal other than that of being in the presence of God by praying the scriptures.

Lectio Divina as a Group Exercise

In the churches of the third world where books are rare, a form of corporate *lectio divina* is becoming common in which a text from the scriptures is pondered by Christians praying together in a group.[1]

This form of *lectio divina* works best in a group of between four and eight people. A group leader coordinates the process and facilitates sharing. The same text from the scriptures is read out three times, followed each time by a period of silence and an opportunity for each member of the group to share the fruit of her or his *lectio*.

The first reading (the text is actually read twice on this occasion) is for the purpose of hearing a word or passage that touches the heart. When the word or phrase is found, it is silently taken in, and gently recited and pondered during the silence which follows. After the silence each person shares which word or phrase has touched his or her heart.

The second reading (by a member of the opposite sex from the first reader) is for the purpose of "hearing" or "seeing" Christ in the text. Each ponders the word that has touched the heart and asks where the word or phrase touches his or her life that day. In other words, how is Christ the word touching his or her own experience, his or her own life? How are the various members of the group seeing or hearing Christ reach out to them through the text? Then, after the silence, each member of the group shares what he or she has "heard" or "seen."

The third and final reading is for the purpose of experiencing Christ "calling us forth" into *doing* or *being*. Members ask

---

[1] This approach to group *lectio divina* was introduced at St. Andrew's Priory by Doug and Norvene Vest. It is used as part of the Benedictine Spirituality for Laity workshop conducted at the Priory each summer.

themselves what Christ in the text is calling them to do or to become today or this week. After the silence, each shares for the last time; and the exercise concludes with each person praying for the person on the right.

Those who regularly practice this method of praying and sharing the scriptures regularly find it to be an excellent way of developing trust within a group; it also is an excellent way of consecrating projects and hopes to Christ before more formal group meetings. A single-sheet summary of this method for group *lectio divina* is appended at the end of this article.

Lectio Divina on Life

In the ancient tradition *lectio divina* was understood as being one of the most important ways in which Christians experience God in creation.[2] After all, the scriptures are part of creation! If one is daily growing in the art of finding Christ in the pages of the Bible, one naturally begins to discover him more clearly in aspects of the other things he has made. This includes, of course, our own personal history.

Our own lives are fit matter for *lectio divina*. Very often our concerns, our relationships, our hopes and aspirations naturally intertwine with our pondering on the scriptures, as has been described above. But sometimes it is fitting to simply sit down and "read" the experiences of the last few days or weeks in our hearts, much as we might slowly read and savor the words of scripture in *lectio divina*. We can attend "with the ear of our hearts" to our own memories, listening for God's gentle presence in the events of our lives. We thus allow ourselves the joy of experiencing Christ reaching out to us through our own memories. Our own personal story becomes "salvation history."

---

[2] Christian life was understood as a gentle oscillation between the poles of *practice* and *contemplation*, as described above; however, contemplation was understood in two ways. First was *theoria physike*, the contemplation of God in creation—God in "the many"; second was *theologia*, the contemplation of God in himself without images or words— God as "The One." *Lectio Divina* was understood as an important part of the contemplation of God in his creation.

For those who are new to the practice of *lectio divina* a group experience of "*lectio* on life" can provide a helpful introduction. An approach that has been used at workshops at St. Andrew's Priory is detailed at the end of this article. Like the experience of *lectio divina* shared in community, this group experience of *lectio* on life can foster relationships in community and enable personal experiences to be consecrated—offered to Christ— in a concrete way.

However, unlike scriptural *lectio divina* shared in community, this group *lectio* on life contains more silence than sharing. The role of group facilitators or leaders is important, since they will be guiding the group through several periods of silence and reflection without the "interruption" of individual sharing until the end of the exercise. Since the experiences we choose to "read" or "listen to" may be intensely personal, it is important in this group exercise to safeguard privacy by making sharing completely optional.

In brief, one begins with restful silence, then gently reviews the events of a given period of time. One seeks an event, a memory, which touches the heart just as a word or phrase in scriptural *lectio divina* does. One then recalls the setting, the circumstances; one seeks to discover how God seemed to be present or absent from the experience. One then offers the event to God and rests for a time in silence.

Conclusion

Lectio divina is an ancient spiritual art that is being rediscovered in our day. It is a way of allowing the scriptures to become again what God intended that they should be—a means of uniting us to himself. In *lectio divina* we discover our own underlying spiritual rhythm. We experience God in a gentle oscillation back and forth between spiritual activity and receptivity, in the movement from practice into contemplation and back again into spiritual practice.

Lectio divina teaches us about the God who truly loves us.

In *lectio divina* we dare to believe that our loving Father continues to extend his embrace to us today. And his embrace is real. In his word we experience ourselves as personally loved by God, as the recipients of a word which he gives uniquely to each of us whenever we turn to him in the scriptures.

Finally, *lectio divina* teaches us about ourselves. In *lectio divina*, we discover that there is no place in our hearts, no interior corner or closet that cannot be opened and offered to God. God teaches us in *lectio divina* what it means to be members of his royal priesthood—a people called to consecrate all of our memories, our hopes and our dreams to Christ.

Lectio Divina
Shared in Community

Listening for the Gentle Touch of Christ the Word
(The Literal Sense)

1. One person reads aloud (twice) the passage of scripture, as others are attentive to some segment that is especially meaningful to them.
2. SILENCE for 1-2 minutes. Each hears and silently repeats a word or phrase that attracts.
3. Sharing aloud: [A word or phrase that has attracted each person]. A simple statement of one or a few words. No elaboration.

How Christ the Word speaks to ME
(The Allegorical Sense)

4. Second reading of same passage by another person.
5. SILENCE for 2-3 minutes. Reflect on "Where does the content of this reading touch my life today?"
6. Sharing aloud: BRIEFLY: "I hear, I see..."

What Christ the Word Invites Me to DO
(The Moral Sense)

7. Third reading by still another person.
8. SILENCE for 2-3 minutes. Reflect on "I believe that God wants me to...today/this week."
9. Sharing aloud: at somewhat greater length the results of each one's reflection. [Be especially aware of what is shared by the person to your right.]
10. After full sharing, pray for the person to your right.

Note: Anyone may pass at any time. If you wish to pray silently, please just state so aloud, and then say Amen when finished.

Lectio on Life
Applying *Lectio Divina* to My Personal Salvation History

Purpose: to apply a method of prayerful reflection to a life/work incident (instead of to a scripture passage).

Listening—Gently Remembering (*Lectio*—Reading)

1. Each person quiets the body and mind: relax, sit comfortably but alert, close eyes, attune to breathing...
2. Each person gently reviews events, situations, sights, encounters that have happened since the beginning of the retreat/or during the last month at work.

Gently Ruminating, Reflecting (*Meditatio*—Meditation)

3. Each person allows the self to focus on one such offering.
   a) Recollect the setting, sensory details, sequence of events, etc.
   b) Notice where the greatest energy seemed to be evoked. Was there a turning point or shift?
   c) In what ways did God seem to be present? To what extent was I aware then? Now?

Prayerful Consecration, Blessing (*Oratio*—Prayer)

4. Offer up to God in prayer the incident and my present reflections. Give it all away to God for now.

Accepting Christ's Embrace; Silent Presence to the Lord (*Contemplatio*—Contemplation)

5. Remain in silence for some period.

**Sharing Our *Lectio* Experience with Each Other
(*Operatio*—Action; Works)**

6. Leader calls the group back into "community."
7. All share briefly (or remain in continuing silence).